Literacy in Context

Language to
analyse, review and comment

John O'Connor

General editors   Joan Ward *and* John O'Connor
Literacy consultant   Lyn Ranson
General consultant   Frances Findlay

CAMBRIDGE
UNIVERSITY PRESS

PUBLISHED BY THE PRESS SYNDICATE OF THE UNIVERSITY OF CAMBRIDGE
The Pitt Building, Trumpington Street, Cambridge, United Kingdom

CAMBRIDGE UNIVERSITY PRESS
The Edinburgh Building, Cambridge CB2 2RU, UK
40 West 20th Street, New York, NY 10011-4211, USA
10 Stamford Road, Oakleigh, VIC 3166, Australia
Ruiz de Alarcón 13, 28014 Madrid, Spain
Dock House, The Waterfront, Cape Town 8001, South Africa

http://www.cambridge.org

First published 2001
Second printing 2001

Printed in the United Kingdom at the University Press, Cambridge

Typeface Delima   *System* QuarkXPress®

A catalogue record for this book is available from the British Library

ISBN 0 521 80554 6 paperback

Prepared for publication by Pentacor Plc

Cover illustration © Bill Butcher

Illustration by Mark Duffin (pp.50, 51)

ACKNOWLEDGEMENTS
The publishers gratefully acknowledge the following for permission to reproduce copyright material.

Textual material Extracts from 'Ivory in the balance' (pp.14, 15) by John Vidal © the *Guardian*, by permission of the *Guardian*; 'The Wolf' leaflet (pp.20, 21), by permission of Born Free Foundation; 'Lydia' advertisement (p.24), by permission of the Christian Children's Fund of Great Britain; *His Dark Materials: Northern Lights* (p.26) by Philip Pullman (1995 edition Scholastic), by permission of Scholastic Ltd.; Supergrass review (pp.32, 33) by Paul Elliott from *Q Magazine* (Planet Syndication), by permission of Planet Syndication; 'New deals on wheels' (pp.38, 39) from *The Big Issue* by Shelley Fannell commissioned by Tina Jackson, by permission of Shelley Fannell; Chicken Run reviews (pp.44, 45) from *BBC News Online*, by permission of the BBC; 'Ali is proclaimed the greatest' (pp.56, 57) from *The Editor*, the *Guardian* 31 December 1999 © the *Guardian*, by permission of the *Guardian*; Jonathan Ross interview with Ridley Scott (p.65) from *Film 2000*, by permission of the BBC; *Escape from Catastrophe* (pp.70, 71) by David Knowles (Knowles Publishing), by permission of David Knowles; *50 Years On* (pp.74, 75) by Roy Hattersley, by permission of Little Brown.

Extracts from *Guardian* reviews (pp.63, 64) first appeared on the Yahoo! movies Web site. The Dunkirk articles (pp. 72, 73, 74, 75) are from BBC News Online; quote by permission of Jaquie Gellman.

Photographs Robbie Williams, Nelson Mandela, Geri Halliwell (pp.8, 9) refs: UPPA, UGL 011821/D-04, UPPA, UIW 16751/A, by permission of Universal Pictorial Press & Agency Ltd.; Pele, Muhammed Ali (p.9) refs: 0162874.jpg, 543688.jpg, by permission of Action Images plc; Ivory poaching (p.15) ref: XP660–448 © Lugmis Dean, by permission of Camera Press, London; Wolves (p.20, 21): refs: B790D 452300-001R © Art Wolfe, B236D 452364-001R © Daniel J Cox, S114D 412499-001 © Rosemary Calvert, by permission of Tony Stone Images; 'Lydia' advertisement (p.24) artwork by permission of Paul Barker Consultancy; Supergrass (p.32) ref: 270574 BRA © Brian Rasic, by permission of Rex Features London; CDs (p.36) ref: TS1648.jpg, by permission of Lester Lefkowitz; Bikes (pp.38, 39) © Andreas Larsson, by permission of Andreas Larsson; Chicken Run (pp.44, 45) ref: 20686, by permission of The Ronald Grant Archive; Monty Python (p.54) ref: RGA Monty Python Parrot SK1.jpg, by permission of The Ronald Grant Archive; Muhammed Ali (p.56) refs: 15838935.jpg, 392259.jpg, 456444.jpg, 544877.jpg, 551105.jpg, by permission of Action Images plc; *Guardian* (p.62) ref: 20686 © Djimon Hounsou, by permission of The Ronald Grant Archive; Ridley Scott (p.65) ref: UPPA UGL 002186/T-23, by permission of Universal Pictorial Press & Agency Ltd.; Dunkirk (pp.70, 73), by permission of The Imperial War Museum; Dunkirk (pp.71, 72) by permission of Bradley Maritime Museum at Ramsgate; Dunkirk (p.72) ref: C1748, HU1860, by permission of The Imperial War Museum; Dunkirk (p.74) by permission of the BBC; Wimbledon (p.75), by permission of Action Images plc.

Every effort has been made to trace copyright holders, but in some cases this has proved impossible. The publishers would be happy to hear from any copyright holder that has not been acknowledged.

Introduction

- Read a piece of text
- Read it again to discover what makes it special
- Check that you understand it
- Focus on key features
- Learn about the language features and practise using them
- Plan and write your own similar piece
- Check it and redraft

Each unit in this book helps you to understand more about a particular kind of writing, learn about its language features and then work towards your own piece of writing in a similar style.

Grammar and punctuation activities, based on the extract, will improve your language skills and take your writing to a higher level.

 **The book at a glance**

The texts

The extracts are based on the National Curriculum reading lists. Each part of the book contains units of extracts and activities at different levels to help you measure your progress.

Each unit includes these sections:

Purpose

This explains exactly what you will read, learn about and write.

Key features

These are the main points to note about the way the extract is written.

Language skills

These activities will improve your grammar and punctuation. They are all based on the extracts. They are organised using the Word, Sentence and Text Level Objectives of the *National Literacy Strategy Framework*.

Planning your own writing

This structured, step-by-step guide will help you to get started, use writing frames and then redraft and improve your work.

Teacher's Portfolio

This includes worksheets for more language practice, revision and homework. Self-assessment charts will help you to judge and record what level you have reached and to set your own targets for improvement.

Contents

Language to analyse

Unit	Text	Key features	Word
1 **What are they like?** Pages 8–13	Newspaper quotes	• Adjectives • Abstract nouns	• Adjectives • Abstract nouns
2 **For and against** Pages 14–19	Writing to analyse an issue Elephants and the ivory trade	• Varied vocabulary • Parenthesis • Presenting both sides of an argument	• Vocabulary
3 **Writing about writing** Pages 20–25	Analysing a text Adopt a wolf	• Organisation into paragraphs • Using quotations • Using evidence from the text	• Tense

Language to review

Unit	Text	Key features	Word
4 **First impressions** Pages 26–31	Writing to review a book 'Lyra and her dæmon' Philip Pullman	• Varied vocabulary • Use of questions • Present tense convention • Use of quotations	• Vocabulary
5 **Checking the notes** Pages 32–37	Writing to review music 'Supergrass' Paul Elliott	• Jargon and specialist terms • Varied sentence structure • Colloquial style • Use of subject knowledge	• Jargon and specialist terms
6 **What's new** Pages 38–43	Reviewing a range of products 'New deals on wheels'	• Up-to-date words • Use of quotes • Style suited to audience	• Alliteration • Rhyme

Spelling	Sentence	Text	Activities
• Negative prefixes	• Apostrophe to show possession	• First person	Writing a self-assessment
• Key subject words	• Parenthesis	• Objective writing	Writing a newspaper article, presenting both sides of an issue
• Rules for adding -ly	• Quotation marks	• Paragraphs • Point–evidence–comment	Analysing a campaign advertisement

Spelling	Sentence	Text	Activities
• Digraphs	• Questions	• Use of the present tense in book reviews • Use of quotations	Reviewing the opening of a novel
• Rules for adding -ly (revision)	• Simple, compound and complex sentences • Conjunctions	• Colloquial style	Writing a music review
• Prefixes	• Speech marks	• Paragraphs and structure	Writing an article to review a range of new products or facilities

Contents

Language to comment

Unit	Text	Key features	Word
7 **Blockbuster** Pages 44–49	Commenting on a new film 'UK *Chicken Run* sets US flapping'	• Wordplay • Quotation • Clear structure	• Wordplay
8 **I wish to make a complaint...** Pages 50–55	Commenting through letters Stripped-off	• Vocabulary to avoid repetition • Layout for formal letters	• Synonyms
9 **In the commentary box** Pages 56–61	Newspaper comments and judgements Sportsperson of the twentieth century	• Exaggeration • Use of quotes • Survey of opinions	• Abstract nouns • Alliteration

Comparing texts

Unit	Text	Key features	Word
10 **From different angles** Pages 62–69	• Online film article (analyse) • Critics' quotes (review) • Interview transcript (comment) *Gladiator* reviews	• Background and summary (analyse) • Simile and metaphor (review) • Commentary and impression (comment)	• Simile and metaphor • Personification
11 **In the news** Pages 70–79	• Online news item • Historical summary (analyse) • Survey of people's opinions (review) • Article on its meaning today (comment) 'Dunkirk remembered'	• Historical background and summary (analyse) • Views and responses (review) • Survey of opinions (comment)	• Adjectives
Glossary Page 80			

Spelling	Sentence	Text	Activities
• *-our* endings	• Quotation marks	• Structure	Writing an online news article
• Negative prefixes	• Time adverbials	• Formal letter layout	Writing a formal letter of complaint
• Compound words • Hyphens	• Colon • Hyperbole	• Surveys • Use of sources	Writing a 'Best of...' article

Spelling	Sentence	Text	Activities
• British and American spellings	• Semicolon	• Genre	Writing to analyse, review and comment on a new TV soap or a new film
• New technological words	• Simple sentences	• Texts that analyse, review and comment	Creating a Web page and link-pages

What are they like?

1 **Purpose**

In this unit you will:

- read some comments written about some famous people
- talk about the way they are written
- write your own self-assessments

» **Subject links:** *media studies, art*

2 **Newspaper quotes**

Describing people's qualities

All of these statements are taken from newspaper reviews. In each one the writer is analysing the qualities of a well-known person or group of people.

'The talented Mr Robbie Williams is not short on ambition…'

'I don't think many people will disagree, when I say that Nelson Mandela – with those rare qualities of patience and forgiveness – was undoubtedly the greatest world figure alive at the dawn of the new millennium…'

'Geri Halliwell's sudden departure was a shock; but it didn't affect the phenomenal Spice Girls' continued success…'

'I find it hard to describe Pele's greatness. He was a magnificent sportsman on and off the field; and his genius was at the heart of the Brazilians' success…'

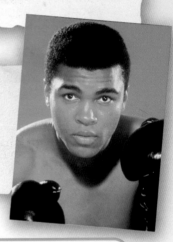

'Most newspapers voted Muhammed Ali sportsperson of the twentieth century. I agree that he was technically skilled, beautiful to watch, original and witty. But I saw his last fights; and they were more about greed and revenge…'

3 ▷ Key features

The writers:
- select appropriate adjectives to describe the people they are writing about
- pinpoint people's qualities by the use of abstract nouns
- express their own viewpoints and judgements

≫
- What are the main talents or achievements for which each of these people is famous: Robbie Williams, Nelson Mandela, Geri Halliwell, Pele and Muhammed Ali?
- According to the quotations, which of the five people was famous for the ability to understand people and for not bearing grudges?
- Which of the five, according to the quotation, had good points and bad?

4 ▷ Language skills

Word

Adjectives are words which describe somebody or something. They give more information about a noun or pronoun.

❶ Which of the personalities pictured were described by these adjectives: *magnificent, greatest, skilled, talented, phenomenal?*

❷ Make a list of five well-known people (perhaps from the world of sport or entertainment) and think up three different adjectives to describe each one. For example, a footballer might be described as *skilful, fast* and *good-looking.* (Another might be *aggressive, greedy* and *talentless*!)

❸ In pairs, read out your lists and challenge each other to:

- work out who the person is (let them know what they are famous for)

- think of a fourth adjective to add to the ones you chose

Abstract nouns are the labels we give to things we cannot touch, see or hear such as emotions, feelings or ideas. People's qualities – such as cleverness or impatience – are all labelled by abstract nouns.

❹ Nelson Mandela is described as having patience. According to the extracts, which of the people pictured have these qualities:

greatness, forgiveness, greed, ambition, success?

❺ Make a list of the qualities needed for success in a particular sport or outdoor activity. Each one should be an abstract noun. Your list might begin with *fitness.*

Spelling

A **prefix** is a group of letters added to the beginning of a word to change its meaning or to create a new word.

When you add a **negative prefix** you do not change the spelling of the root word.

One of the newspaper comments begins, *I don't think many people will disagree... . Disagree* is formed by adding the prefix *dis-* to the root word *agree. Dis-* is an example of a negative prefix.

❶ Add a negative prefix to these words: *appear, appoint, natural, satisfied, legal, regular, obedient, mortal.*

Sentence

The **apostrophe** (') is a punctuation mark with two different uses:

- to show that a letter or group of letters has been missed out
- to show possession (or ownership)

When you are describing someone's qualities, you will probably need to use the apostrophe for possession. For example, you might write about *Nelson Mandela's courage* or *Robbie Williams' greatness.*

1 All of these examples are in the newspaper extracts. Write them out with the apostrophes in the correct places and then check to see if you were right.

> *Geri Halliwells sudden departure*
>
> *the phenomenal Spice Girls continued success*
>
> *Peles greatness*
>
> *the Brazilians success*

In pairs, talk about the rule that you followed in deciding where to place the apostrophe. If you are in any doubt, there is an easy-to-remember, three-step rule for using the apostrophe for possession. It appears in the Teacher's Portfolio.

Text

When you write something from your own viewpoint, using the pronoun *I*, we say that you are writing in the **first person** of the verb: *I believe, I said, we thought, we knew.* The first person is useful when you want to show the reader that you are expressing your own judgements.

1 Look back at the extracts and find these phrases which are written in the first person. Which personal opinion follows each one?

> *I say that...*
>
> *I find it hard...*
>
> *I agree...*

11

5 ▶ Planning your own writing

This is the opening of a Year 7 student's own assessment of their progress in English.

I have enjoyed writing stories this term, but I'm not very good at expressing my own opinions.
I probably ought to read more.
My spelling is quite good, though I often have problems with longer, unusual words. I have started to keep a diary and...

Write your own self-assessment of something you are learning to do.

▶▶ STARTING POINTS

- You could write about something you are doing in school.
- You might prefer to write about something which has nothing to do with school: perhaps you are attending karate classes or learning how to keep tarantulas.
- Write about a hundred words and don't try to cover everything.

▶▶ CLUES FOR SUCCESS

- Select adjectives to describe yourself accurately.
- Use carefully chosen abstract nouns when you write about your qualities.
- Write in the first person.

▶▶ REDRAFTING AND IMPROVING

In groups or pairs, look closely at your own and other people's first drafts. Make suggestions for improving, editing or adding more detail. If you have used a word-processor, the redrafting process will be much simpler.

Now think about your own final version. How can your writing be improved even further? Check that:

- your personality has come across
- you have involved the reader
- you have chosen words carefully, especially the adjectives and abstract nouns which described your qualities
- you have organised different sections of your writing into paragraphs

WRITING FRAME

You might find it helpful to use this structure.

Paragraph and contents	Example	Language features
1 Introduce yourself and the activity you are going to write about.	*I have been learning to play the guitar for six months...*	first person
2 Which qualities are needed for success?	*You have to have a great deal of patience...*	abstract nouns
3 How would you describe yourself?	*I am fairly musical...*	adjectives
4 List your achievements so far.	*I have learned to...*	

6 Looking back

- **Adjectives** and **abstract nouns** have to be chosen carefully if you want to describe yourself, or someone else, accurately.

- Write in the **first person** when you want to give your own viewpoint; the third person is used when you are writing about someone else.

For and against

In this unit you will:

- read a newspaper article which analyses the arguments for and against a topical question
- decide what makes that kind of article successful
- write your own for-and-against article

≫ **Subject links:** *geography, science, art*

2 ▷ Writing to analyse an issue

Elephants and the ivory trade

In the 1980s many people became concerned that African elephants were being killed in large numbers for their ivory tusks, which were then sold abroad for high prices. To protect the elephants, this ivory trade was banned in 1989. But is it now time for the ban to be dropped? This newspaper article sets out the arguments for and against.

Ivory ban in the balance

The governments of some countries support the killing of a limited number of African elephants. But conservationists say that numbers are already too low and the future of the elephant is not secure. Almost all
5   conservationists argue that the ban should remain in place. They predict that, if it were lifted, poachers would take this as a signal that they could return to ways that halved Africa's stock of elephants in the 1980s.

    Many British conservationists, among them Alan
10   Thornton of the Environmental Investigation Agency, believe that counting methods are not precise enough and that the size of the elephant population could have been overestimated. More importantly, they point out that elephant numbers today are fifteen per cent less than they
15   were ten years ago. The elephant is still very much an endangered species.

Some British and American conservationists oppose any killing of elephants or the sale of elephant products. Greed, they argue, is why elephants are killed. They say that the world does not need to add to the destruction of wildlife over the last hundred years. If elephants are causing a problem, destroying crops, for instance, solutions can be found such as cross-border game parks where elephants can roam at will.

However, the governments of South Africa, Botswana, Zimbabwe, Namibia and Malawi say they have enough – or too many – elephants. In some cases stocks are increasing by up to five per cent a year. They want the right to trade with other countries in ivory as they once did, because they believe it is the best way to maintain a stable elephant population – and earn an income.

Elephant trade, they argue, has long been a part of the culture of many communities. People should have the right to profit from wildlife just as people who catch fish profit from the sea. They resent what they see as conservationists' emotional arguments and the way in which foreign campaigners have tried to dictate how poor countries in Africa should behave towards the elephant. They say that the only way to protect the people who live in rural areas is to allow them to return to their elephant trade.

They also point out that, if elephant populations are allowed to grow (numbers can double within sixteen years), many will die in times of drought. Sometimes elephant populations 'crash' because there are too many trying to use an area. To kill a few elephants humanely is better, they suggest, than watching nature take its toll.

John Vidal

3 > Key features

The writer:
- uses varied vocabulary
- uses parenthesis
- presents both sides of the argument fairly

- Which groups want to keep the ban on the trade in ivory and which groups want to see the ban lifted?
- What would you pick out as the three main arguments in favour of keeping the ban, according to this article?
- What are the three main arguments in favour of lifting it?

4 Language skills

Word

Good writers develop a wide vocabulary. This allows them to say exactly what they mean and also adds variety to their writing.

A good example of **varied vocabulary** is the way this writer chooses different words to mean *say*.

❶ In the opening paragraph we find, *But conservationists say that numbers are already too low...* Look through the rest of the article and pick out the different words the writer chooses instead of *say*. You will find them in the following checklist:

> *suggest, predict, argue, believe, point out, declare, comment, observe, assert, contend, claim, allege, stress, underline, repeat, highlight*

❷ Pick three words from the list which the writer has not used and include them in sentences of your own. For example, you might write:

> *My brother commented that the ticket prices were too high.*

Spelling

When you are writing about issues like this, it is important to spell key words correctly – otherwise readers will not take your arguments seriously.

Look out for:

- the *n* in the middle of *environment* and *government*
- the odd spelling of *species*
- the silent *g* in *campaign*

❶ Talk in pairs about ways in which you might remember these spellings. (For example, to remember the *n* in *environmental*, you might think of a heavy metal guitarist, Ron Mental...)

Sentence

If we add a word or phrase to a sentence, putting it inside commas, brackets or dashes, we say that the word or phrase is in **parenthesis**. (To pronounce it, put the stress on the *ren*.)

❶ Words in parenthesis are added in order to explain something or expand on a point that has been made. Look back through the article and find the uses of dashes and brackets for parenthesis (lines 28 and 45). What important point do the phrases in parenthesis add in each case?

2 Commas can also be used for parenthesis. Find the examples in paragraph 3 (lines 19 and 23).

3 Use commas, brackets or dashes to add phrases in parenthesis to the middle of each of the following sentences. For example:

Original sentence: *Thunderbolts were sent by Jupiter.*

Add *they believed*, using commas.

New sentence: *Thunderbolts, they believed, were sent by Jupiter.*

- Original sentence: *Otter hunting is cruel and inhumane.*

  Add *they argue*, using commas.

- Original sentence: *Mrs Cartwright was also at the meeting.*

  Add *the new manager*, using brackets.

- Original sentence *The problem was more interesting than I had expected.*

  Add *and much more difficult*, using dashes.

Make up some examples of your own and challenge someone to complete them.

4 Draft a simple rule to explain where you should place the commas, brackets and dashes in parenthesis.

You might begin: *When you want to use commas in parenthesis, you place them...*

Text

When someone tries to present all sides of an argument fairly, without seeming to support one side or another, we say they are being **neutral** or **objective**.

1 In pairs, talk about the ways in which the writer of the article manages to present both sides of the argument fairly. These activities will help you:

- Count the number of paragraphs devoted to arguments in favour of keeping the ban and then count how many there are against it. What do you notice?

- Look at the use of statistics to support the two sides (see paragraphs 1, 2, 4 and 6). Are there roughly the same number on each side?

- Study the way the writer quotes people on both sides who have 'expert' or 'first-hand' experience (paragraphs 2 and 4). Again, is there a fair balance?

5 ▷ Planning your own writing

Pick an issue that interests you and write a newspaper article which sets out the arguments for and against, in a balanced and objective way.

▷▷ STARTING POINTS

You might choose to write about the arguments for and against:

● changing a school rule (perhaps to do with uniform or attendance)

● building something locally (such as a new sports stadium)

● banning something – or lifting an existing ban (for example on a sport considered cruel)

● changing your environment (for example, making your town centre a traffic-free pedestrian zone)

▷▷ CLUES FOR SUCCESS

● Choose an issue that really interests you and for which you can find something out.

● Think carefully about varying the expressions for *say*.

● Use parentheses (commas, brackets and dashes) to add further facts or phrases such as *they argue*.

● Present both sides of the argument fairly.

▶▶ WRITING FRAME

This is how the writer structured the article about the ivory ban. It might help you to plan your own writing.

OOOOOOOOOOOOOOOOOOOOOOOOOOOO

Writing about an issue: for and against

Paragraphs and structure	Content
1 Introducing the issues	• one sentence stating the case 'for' • one sentence stating the case 'against'
2, 3 The arguments 'for'	• the main argument 'for' • a specific piece of evidence • quoting 'an authority' or people with first-hand experience • further points
4, 5, 6 The arguments 'against'	• the main argument 'against' • quoting 'an authority' or people with first-hand experience • further points

▶▶ REDRAFTING AND IMPROVING

Look carefully at your latest version. How can it be improved? Check that you have:

- chosen vocabulary which is varied and helps to get your points across clearly
- spelt the key words correctly
- included fair and balanced arguments on both sides
- punctuated accurately, including any punctuation for parenthesis

6 ▷ Looking back

When you are analysing an issue, writing about the arguments for and against, it is important to:

- present both sides of the argument **objectively**
- introduce people's different viewpoints using **varied vocabulary**
- include details in **parenthesis**, correctly punctuated

Writing about writing

1 ▷ **Purpose**

In this unit you will:
- read a piece of writing which analyses a text
- decide what makes that kind of writing successful
- produce your own piece of analytical writing

≫ **Subject links:** *science, art*

2 ▷ **Analysing a text**

Adopt a wolf

This extract is taken from a leaflet published by Operation Wolf, a campaign to help wolves in their fight against extinction.

THE WOLF

Once the most widespread mammal in the northern hemisphere, the wolf now stands on the brink of extinction in many countries. In others it has gone – possibly forever. 5

Threats to survival
- Persecution by people
- Habitat destruction
- Competition with people for larger prey
- Hybridisation (cross-breeding between wolves and wild dogs)

In Britain it is over 250 years since the forests provided the last refuge for wolves trying to escape the all-out war that was waged against them.

What is it about this animal that, in some people, arouses such intense feelings of fear and hate? Yet those people 10 who have studied this species hold wolves in deep respect, admiring their intelligence, devotion to family and skilled hunting abilities.

Buried deep in many people's subconscious is the 'fictional' wolf many of us were brought up to fear – the 15 villain of myth and fairy tale. Add to this the competition between humans and wolves for food and land, and the result has been a long-running, one-sided battle which has sadly made the wolf one of nature's most misunderstood and persecuted animals. 20

Family life
Wolves live in a tightly-knit group called a 'pack', bound by friendship, loyalty and need. They enjoy playing together and the security the pack offers. Pups are the focal point for the whole family with uncles and aunts all helping to provide food and care. Intelligent and friendly, the wolf is 25 one of nature's most socially developed animals.

Analysing the leaflet

This is one Year 9 student's written analysis of the Operation Wolf campaign leaflet. The student had been set the question 'How does the leaflet try to change people's opinions about wolves?'

The leaflet says that some people have 'feelings of fear and hate' about wolves, but then goes on to say that people who have studied wolves actually have feelings of 'deep respect' for these animals. It is saying that, when most people think of wolves, they think of the 'fictional' wolf and, if they knew what wolves were really like, they would admire them, not hate them.

The writer selects information that gives a good view of wolves, saying that they live in 'a tightly-knit family group' – where the term 'family' is usually applied to humans. Words such as 'friendship, loyalty and need' are used to create a positive image of wolves. Again, these descriptions are more often used of humans, so it makes people think that wolves are more like humans.

I think that this leaflet will be successful for some readers, and the pictures also help a lot. They show the wolves looking harmless and more like dogs – which would probably change some dog-owners' opinions about wolves.

The description of the wolf's family life is also very effective in changing people's opinions, but there will always be some people who hate wolves so much that they will ignore this leaflet as soon as they read the title.

3 > Key features

The writer:
- organises the writing in clearly structured paragraphs
- includes correctly punctuated quotations
- uses evidence from the text

>>
- Which quotations to do with people's feelings about wolves does the writer select from the leaflet? (They have been included in her first paragraph.)
- Which words does the writer quote in her second paragraph to show that the leaflet puts forward a positive image of wolves?
- What does the writer say in her concluding paragraph about the different kinds of people who will read the leaflet?

4 > Language skills

Word

A verb's tense is the form of the verb which shows *when* something happens – either in the past or the present or the future. This kind of critical writing always has most of its verbs in the **present tense**. For example, the second paragraph opens with *The writer selects information...*, as though it is happening now. It is a convention (a custom that people accept and follow) to use the present tense when you are analysing a piece of writing.

❶ Pick out the present-tense verbs in these phrases from the passage:

> *The leaflet says that some people have 'feelings of fear and hate' about wolves, but then goes on...*

> *It is saying that, when most people think of wolves...*

> *The writer selects information that gives a good view of wolves...*

Spelling

There are three rules for adding *-ly*, to form an adverb.

Rule one: Most English adverbs are formed simply by adding *-ly* to the end of the adjective (such as *tight – tightly*, in paragraph 2).

❶ Make a list of other adverbs which are formed simply by adding *-ly* to the adjective. Start off with *quick – quickly*.

❷ What happens when the adjective already ends in a single *-l*? Write down these three adjectives: *actual*, *real* and *usual*. Now write down the three adverbs which are formed from them (you will find them all in the student's writing on page 21). What do you notice about the spelling of the new endings? Complete the second rule:

Rule two: Even if the adjective already ends in a single *-l*, ...

❸ There is one adverb in this passage which does not follow the basic rule: *probably*. Which adjective does it come from? Complete this third rule:

Rule three: If the adjective ends in *-able* or *-ible*, you have to ... to turn it into an adverb.

Sentence

Quotation marks (' ') – also known as inverted commas or speech marks – are used in the punctuation of speech. They can also show that a word or phrase is being quoted from somewhere else.

1 Look carefully at the opening sentence of the student's writing. Which words has the writer quoted from the original leaflet about wolves? How can you tell?

2 List all the other words and phrases that the writer has quoted.

3 Write a rule for how to use quotation marks in this way. Make sure that your rule explains exactly where the quotation marks should go and how they should be written. You could begin: *When you quote a word or phrase from a piece of writing…*

Text

Paragraphs are blocks of sentences linked together by one main idea or subject.

1 How many paragraphs are there in the student's piece of writing?

2 Write a 'topic heading' for each paragraph to show what it is about. For example, the first paragraph might be headed: *Introduction: a summary of the leaflet's main points.*

When you are analysing a text, it is important to support your points with **evidence**.

After you have quoted the evidence, it is then interesting to add a comment. Look, for example, at the beginning of the student's second paragraph:

The writer selects information that gives a good view of wolves,	● make a **point**
saying that they live in 'a tightly-knit family group'	● quote the **evidence** to support it
– where the term 'family' is usually applied to humans.	● make a **comment** on the quotation

3 This method is called **point–evidence–comment**. To understand how it works, discuss the following questions in pairs:

● How does the evidence help to support the writer's point here?

● What does the comment add? Which extra point or explanation is included in the comment?

4 Find the point, the evidence and the comment in paragraph 3.

23

5 ▷ Planning your own writing

This is a campaign advertisement for the Christian Children's Fund of Great Britain from the teen magazine *J 17*. Write about the ways in which it attempts to persuade you to be a sponsor.

▶▶ STARTING POINTS

Look carefully at:

- the way the writing addresses you, the reader, directly

- the strong, *emotive* language (words and phrases which can produce feelings such as pity or disgust)

- the use of vivid descriptions and impressive details

- the organisation of the paragraphs (some devoted to a description of the harsh conditions, some telling you how your money will help)

- the way the text (including the writing around the border) is combined with the images (the main picture and the ones at the bottom)

▶▶ CLUES FOR SUCCESS

- Make detailed notes first.

- Select evidence carefully (points and quotes from the advertisement).

- Then organise your notes into paragraphs.

- Make sure that your analysis has a clear introduction.

throughout the developing world and Eastern Europe to help bring healthcare, education and eventual self-sufficiency to children and communities in need. Support is always given on the basis of poverty, and regardless of race, sex or religion

Children's Fund of Great Britain is a humanitarian, non-denominational registered charity working with locally owned, long-term pro

For Lidia, life began on the scrap heap...

The scrap heap on the outskirts of Lidia's home town in Bolivia is not a place you would want to visit. If the foul stench doesn't stop you in your tracks then the sight of the hundreds of rats and the putrid waste would be enough to turn any stomach.

Unbelievable as it may seem, this scrap heap like so many others worldwide, has become home for thousands of families who live in appalling poverty, surviving by scavenging for bits of food to eat and the few scrap items they can sell on the streets.

Children, barefoot and in rags, scramble over the broken glass, tins and other debris in their pathetic search. Many will succumb to disease and infection and many die.

Yet just £15 a month could sponsor a child and give them a very different life full of hope, good health and a bright future. You can help to make that happen.

By sponsoring a child through CCF you can ensure that they grow up with enough to eat, clothes to wear and with provision for their health and educational needs.

Through your help and care children like Lidia will have a real chance of a decent future for themselves and their communities.

As you read these few words, other vulnerable children throughout the world will be trying to beat each other to whatever shreds of food may lie amongst the squalor.

Please become a sponsor today - it could be one of the most important and rewarding things you ever do. Thank you.

...with your sponsorship it need not end there

Just £15 a month can give a child a decent future.

Your sponsorship can be for as long as you wish – six months, a year, or until the child leaves school. You will receive a photo of the child, details of his or her family background, regular progress reports and letters from the child you are supporting.

Yes, I would like to sponsor a child

DMR21

Send to Christian Children's Fund, 4 Bath Place, Rivington Street, London EC2A 3DR or CCF GB, FREEPOST WC4509, London EC2B 3FN (no stamp needed in UK) Tel: 0171 799 8191

My first monthly payment of £15 is enclosed by cheque/Postal Order
(cheques made payable to CCF GB)

I would prefer to pay £15 by Visa / Mastercard /Access / Amex / Diners

Card No:

Expiry Date:

Valid from:

Signature for card payments

Please send my information pack today

I cannot sponsor a child but would like to donate a gift of £

Charity Reg. 087545

I prefer a ☐ boy ☐ girl ☐ either
In any country ☐ OR

Eastern Europe ☐
Bulgaria ☐
Romania ☐
Russia ☐

Latin America ☐
Asia ☐
Africa ☐
Caribbean ☐

Name:
Address:
Postcode:

CCF

WRITING FRAME

You might decide to structure your piece in five paragraphs, like this, backing up your points with the quotations that have been suggested (as well as others that you can find for yourself).

How does the advertisement attempt to persuade you to be a sponsor?

Paragraph and content	Possible opening phrase	Example of evidence
1 Introduction	Throughout this advertisement, the reader is addressed directly...	'not a place you would want to visit...'
2 Emotive language	Emotive language is employed right from the beginning...	'life began on the scrap heap...'
3 Vivid descriptions and impressive details	The writer has selected some extremely impressive phrases...	'the sight of hundreds of rats and the putrid waste...'
4 Organisation of paragraphs	In order to persuade the reader and construct a strong argument...	Paragraphs 1 to 3, compared with paragraphs 4 to 6
5 The combination of text and image	Like the text, the images are simple and powerful...	The main picture, next to the text, is of Lidia herself

---

REDRAFTING AND IMPROVING

Look carefully at your analysis.
Check that you have:

- planned carefully what is to go in each paragraph
- quoted evidence from the advertisement to back up your statements
- used the point–evidence–comment system
- kept your main verbs in the present tense

6 Looking back

- Use the **present tense** when you are writing an analysis of a text.
- Structure your writing in clearly organised **paragraphs**.
- Use the **point–evidence–comment** system to make your analysis interesting and well argued.

First impressions

1 ▷ **Purpose**

In this unit you will:
- read the opening of a book
- read a review of the opening
- learn how a review is written
- write your own book review

▷▷ **Subject links:** *literature, art*

2 ▷ **Writing to review a book**

This is the opening of a novel called Northern Lights *by Philip Pullman. The strange word* dæmon *is pronounced the same as* demon: *'dee-mon'.*

Lyra and her dæmon

Lyra and her dæmon moved through the darkening Hall, taking care to keep to one side, out of sight of the kitchen. The three great tables that ran the length of the Hall were laid already, the silver and the glass catching what little light there was, and the long benches were pulled out ready for the guests. Portraits of former Masters hung high up in the gloom along the walls. Lyra reached the dais and looked back at the open kitchen door and, seeing no one, stepped up beside the high table. The places here were laid with gold, not silver, and the fourteen seats were not oak benches but mahogany chairs with velvet cushions.

Lyra stopped beside the Master's chair and flicked the biggest glass gently with a fingernail. The sound rang clearly through the Hall.

'You're not taking this seriously,' whispered her dæmon. 'Behave yourself.'

Her dæmon's name was Pantalaimon, and he was currently in the form of a moth, a dark brown one so as not to show up in the darkness of the Hall.

Reviewing the opening

This is what Tim, a Year 7 student, wrote about the opening of Northern Lights.

This opening really makes me want to read on. There are all sorts of mysterious questions that I would like the answer to. Who is Lyra? Where is this dark Hall? And my main question: what is a dæmon? This one has the strange name Pantalaimon. It seems to be some kind of creature that can turn itself into different animals, because the narrator says, 'he was currently in the form of a moth'. Whatever it is, it can talk, and seems to know Lyra well because it tells her to behave herself.

Philip Pullman builds up the atmosphere brilliantly. He writes about 'the darkening Hall' and describes how the small amount of light catches the silver and glass. It must be a very rich place: people on the high table eat off gold plates. It made me wonder whether the story was happening now, in the twenty-first century, or in some other time. Certainly people have been using the Hall for a long time, because it says that 'Portraits of former Masters hung high up in the gloom along the walls'.

I think Lyra and Pantalaimon are not supposed to be in the Hall. I can tell this because they take care to keep out of sight of the kitchen. Also the dæmon talks in a whisper and has made himself dark brown so as not to show up in the darkness.

I have the feeling that Lyra intends to watch the meal secretly. She doesn't want anyone to know she is there. To me she seems suspicious and wants to find out what is going on.

I am sure I will enjoy this book. Lyra seems an interesting heroine and I am dying to know what a dæmon is.

3 ▷ Key features

Tim, the writer of the review:

- varies his vocabulary
- uses questions to pick out some key points
- always uses the present tense when he is relating incidents from the book
- supports his impressions with quotations from the text

- What is the most important question that Tim wants an answer to?
- Which quotes does Tim use when he is writing about the novel's atmosphere in paragraph 2?
- What has Tim learned about Lyra from her behaviour in the hall?

4 ⟩ Language skills

Word

It helps to have a **wide vocabulary** when you are writing a review. For example, you need to find different ways in which to introduce your impressions. It becomes boring if every sentence starts with *I think that…*.

Look at the different ways in which Tim has introduced his impressions of *Northern Lights*:

> *It seems to be…*
> *It must be…*
> *I think…*
> *I have the feeling that…*
> *To me…*
> *I am sure…*

1 Find and write down the sentences which open with those phrases.

2 Here are other ways in which you could introduce your impressions. Complete each of them with a statement about the opening of *Northern Lights*.

> *I get the impression that…*
> *In my opinion…*
> *I wonder if…*
> *I am guessing that…*
> *Perhaps…*

Spelling

Two letters used to make a single sound are called a **digraph**.

According to Philip Pullman, the author of *Northern Lights*, dæmon should be pronounced like the English word *demon* ('dee-mon'). You will notice that dæmon contains two letters, *a* and *e*, joined up to make one: æ.

When we use two letters to represent one sound, we call it a digraph. In English we have vowel digraphs (such as the *oa* in *road*) and consonant digraphs. The most common consonant digraphs in English are: *th* (in *this* and *thin*), *sh* (in *shop*) and *ch* (in *church*).

1 Write down examples of words which include the following consonant digraphs: *ph, gh, ng, ck, dg*.

2 There are several different ways of spelling the 'ee' sound in *demon*. Here are some examples. Find one other example for each spelling: *receive, siege, bead, seen, machine, ecology, foetus*.

3 Which famous Roman has a name which is sometimes spelt with the digraph æ?

Sentence

A simple sentence can be a **statement**, a **question**, a **command** or an **exclamation**.

Most of Tim's sentences are statements. But he makes interesting use of questions too.

1 How many question sentences are there in Tim's opening paragraph?

2 Tim's questions help to pick out the key mysteries facing the reader at the opening of *Northern Lights*. Write down the questions that Tim wants answers to.

3 What other mysteries does Philip Pullman create at the beginning of his book? Add a further question or two of your own.

Text

When you relate events from a book, always use the **present tense**.

Philip Pullman's story is told in the past tense:

Lyra and her dæmon ***moved***...

*The three great tables that **ran** the length of the hall **were laid** already*...

But if you are writing a review, and you want to refer to these events, you have to use the present tense:

I like the opening of the book, when Lyra and her dæmon ***move*** *through the Hall*...

*Philip Pullman describes how the tables which **run** the length of the Hall **are** already laid*...

The only exception is when you are quoting the writer's exact words. Then you keep to whichever tense the writer used:

*...the narrator says, 'he **was** currently in the form of a moth...'*

1 Reread the fourth paragraph of Tim's review (*I have the feeling*...) where he is describing Lyra's behaviour. Pick out the verbs that he has put into the present tense. (Ignore *to watch* and *to know*: these are **infinitives**.)

If you include the exact words from a book you are reviewing, you are using a **quotation**. Quotations are sometimes known more simply as '*quotes*'.

Tim uses three quotes in his review. Find the quotes which he uses:

- to show how he knows that the dæmon can change into different animals
- to give an example of the way the writer creates atmosphere
- to show how he knows that the Hall has been in use for a long time

5 ▷ Planning your own writing

Write your own review of the opening of a novel.

▷▷ STARTING POINT

Choose a book that someone else has recommended, but that you have not yet read yourself. Base your review on the first page or two, or the first chapter if it is quite short.

▷▷ CLUES FOR SUCCESS

You will find it more fun to write a review on an opening that you have enjoyed.

- First of all make a list in note form of all the main facts that the writer gives you in the opening of the book. Who are the characters? Where is the story set?

- Then decide what questions have been left unanswered. For example, do you know where the main character comes from or what she or he is trying to do?

- Note down some impressions and try to work out what you think might be going on.

- Make some predictions about what might happen later in the story. You might say what it is you think you are going to enjoy about it.

WRITING FRAME

If you need further help, here is a writing frame based on Tim's review of the opening of *Northern Lights*.

Book review: *Northern Lights*

Paragraph and content	Possible opening phrase
1 Introduction: • some questions to be answered	*There are all sorts of mysterious questions that I would like the answer to…*
2 Descriptions: • the setting and the atmosphere	*The writer builds up the atmosphere brilliantly…* *He writes about (quote '_____')*
3 Impressions	*I think…* *I can tell this because…*
4 Deductions (things you can work out)	*I have the feeling that…* *To me…*
5 Predictions (what is likely to happen)	*I'm sure I will enjoy…*

REDRAFTING AND IMPROVING

Look carefully at your first draft. Check that you have:

● varied the way in which you introduce your impressions

● used the present tense when you are relating incidents from the book

● used quotes to help explain your impressions

6 Looking back

● Your **vocabulary** is the range of words that you use. Try to make it as varied as possible.

● **Tense** is the form of the verb which tells us when the action is taking place. When you are describing what happens in a story, relate it in the **present tense**.

● A **quotation** is an author's exact words. Use quotes from the book to back up the points you are making.

Checking the notes

1 ▷ Purpose

In this unit you will:

- read a review of a music album
- learn about the way it is written
- write your own music review

》》 Subject link: *music*

Location: http://freespace.virgin.net/david.wilcox/supergrass

What's New?   What's Cool?   Handbook   Net Search   Net Directory

2 ▷ Writing to review music

Supergrass

This review of a new Supergrass album, written by Paul Elliott, appeared in Q *magazine. It was taken from the Supergrass site, 'The Strange Ones' (http://freespace.virgin.net/david. wilcox/supergrass)*

3 ▷ Key features

The writer:

- uses special vocabulary to do with rock and pop
- varies the writing with different types of sentence structure
- has a colloquial style
- uses his knowledge of the subject to express interesting and informed opinions

The Band	The Look
The Music	The Tabs
The Tour	The Links
The Press	The Mail
The Goods	The FAQ
The Lyrics	The Club

The Strange Ones Supergrass Site

SUPERGRASS

Supergrass

PARLOPHONE 522 0562

Spielberg apparently wanted to turn them into The Monkees via a television series, but Supergrass are making music comparable to The Beach Boys and The Beatles. There is, in fact, more Beatlery here than on any of Oasis's albums.

Supergrass songs, like those of their heroes, are fit to burst with good ideas. The first song here, 'Moving', is moody, a bit glam-rock, a bit funky, and it all fits together seamlessly. When they jam a little on 'Born Again', the sound is as good as Pink Floyd in their prime.

This is ageless pop music. 'Shotover Hill's sunshiny harmonies carry echoes of 'Pet Sounds'. 'Beautiful People' – sung by bassist Micky Quinn – is their very own 'The Ballad of John and Yoko'.

Of course, Supergrass are not really as good as The Beatles. Nobody is, probably, but that's not the point. These little herberts from Oxford get closer than most.

Paul Elliott

- According to the review, what did the film director Steven Spielberg want to do with Supergrass?
- Which three groups are Supergrass compared with in the opening paragraph?
- What is the reviewer's opinion of the Beatles, and how does he think Supergrass compares with them?

4 Language skills

Word

Jargon is the name we give to the special words and phrases used by particular groups of people who share the same job or interest. Jargon words can also be called **specialist terms**.

Some examples of jargon in the Supergrass review will probably be understood only by people interested in rock and pop. *Glam-rock*, for example, is a kind of music popular in the 1970s.

❶ Talk in pairs about these examples of specialist language or jargon and decide how you would explain their meanings to somebody who knew nothing about rock and pop: *funky, jam, bassist.*

Spelling

As you learned on page 22, the usual way to turn an adjective into an adverb is to add *-ly*. Here are some revision questions.

❶ What happens to the spelling of adjectives which end in a single *-l*?

❷ What happens to those ending in *-e*?

To remind you, here are some examples of adverbs from the Supergrass review.

Adjective	What to look out for	+ *-ly* becomes the adverb
apparent		*apparently*
real	ends in a single *-l*	*really*
probable	ends in *-e*	*probably*

Sentence

Sentences can be structured in three ways: you can have **simple sentences**, **compound sentences** and **complex sentences**.

Simple sentences say just one thing:

This is ageless pop music.

If you join two or more simple sentences together with *or, and* or *but*, you get a compound sentence:

Sentence a		Sentence b
Nobody is, probably,	*but*	*that's not the point.*

If you join two or more sentences together with a word which shows how they are connected in meaning, you get a complex sentence:

	Sentence a	Sentence b
When	they jam on 'Born Again',	the sound is as good as Pink Floyd in their prime.

The words which joined the two parts of the sentence in these examples (*but* and *when*) are called **conjunctions**.

If you can vary the type of sentence you use, your writing will become much more interesting and you will be able to express your ideas more clearly.

❶ Add a conjunction to each of these pairs of sentences to form a complex sentence. Here is a list of conjunctions to choose from: *after, although, as, because, before, if, since, though, unless, until, when, while.*

Conjunction	Sentence a	Sentence b
	Spielberg offered Supergrass a TV series	they turned him down
	their music sounds like the Beatles	it will last a long time
	this album doesn't have a proper title	it is bound to be successful

Text

Informal, everyday speech and writing are sometimes called **colloquial** English. Writers often use colloquial language if they want to sound relaxed and informal, as though they are speaking to the reader as a friend who shares the same interests.

The Supergrass review includes several examples of colloquial language:

- ***fit to burst** with good ideas*
- ***a bit** funky*
- *These **little herberts** from Oxford*

If those three examples of colloquial language were redrafted into formal English, they might come out as:

- *Supergrass songs are **absolutely full** of good ideas.*
- *The first song is **rather** funky.*
- *These **young men** from Oxford get closer than most.*

❶ In pairs, talk about the differences between the colloquial and formal versions. Which ones do you think are more appropriate for a review in a popular music magazine? Why? Write a sentence or two to explain your choice.

❷ Colloquial writing will sometimes involve inventing new words. Write down what you think *Beatlery* means.

5 ❯ Planning your own writing

Write your own music review. Pick an album that you know well, or one that has just been released, so that you can look at other reviews to get some ideas.

❯❯ STARTING POINT

Choose a band (or a soloist, or an orchestra) which has a Web site and look up some of the reviews of their latest album.

❯❯ CLUES FOR SUCCESS

- Notice the kind of language the reviewers use. Is it colloquial? Does it contain much jargon?

- Are there comparisons with other bands?

- Do the writers vary their sentence structures to make the review interesting to read?

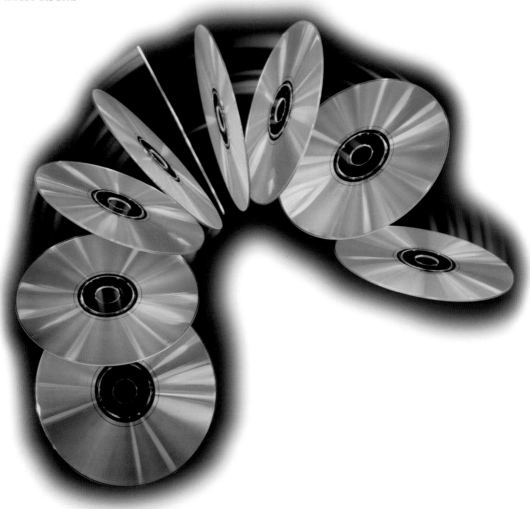

>> WRITING FRAME

If you need further help, here is a writing frame
for a review about a new band, Ginger Baby.

Music review: Ginger Baby

Paragraph and content	Possible opening phrase
1 An opening statement: something special about this particular album	*In this new album, Drinking from the Hot Tap...*
2 Something about particular songs (or pieces of music)	*Ginger Baby's first song, 'Sunday' is...*
3 Some comparisons with other bands (or soloists or orchestras)	*Hambidge's singing carries echoes of...*
4 A general summing-up point	*So how good are they...?*

>> REDRAFTING AND IMPROVING

Look at your work again. Check that
you have:

- made the right choice about
  whether to use formal or colloquial
  English

- used jargon or specialist terms only
  where they are necessary

- varied the kinds of sentence you
  have used

- used your knowledge of the
  subject to make interesting and
  well-informed points

6 > Looking back

- People who share the same job
  or interest often use **jargon** or
  specialist terms.

- **Sentences** can be **simple**,
  compound or **complex**. Your
  writing will be much more
  precise and also more
  interesting to read if you vary
  the kinds of sentence you use.
  The words which join two or
  more parts of the sentence are
  called **conjunctions**.

- **Colloquial** English is informal.
  You have to decide when it is
  appropriate to use colloquial,
  rather than formal, English.

What's new?

1 ▷ Purpose

In this unit you will:

- read a review of new methods of travel in the city
- learn about the way the review is written
- write your own review of a new range of products

➤➤ **Subject links:** *technology, art*

2 ▷ Reviewing a range of products

New deals on wheels

This review of alternative city transport, written by Shelley Fannell, appeared in The Big Issue.

3 ▷ Key features

The writer:

- uses up-to-date words which catch the reader's attention
- includes quotations from people who use the products
- gears the style of writing to a particular audience

SNAP SHOT
New deals on wheels

As pollution levels rise and urban traffic hits gridlock, eco-conscious city-travellers are seeking out less traditional ways to get around town. They're funky, fun and foot-powered. Beats sitting in a traffic jam.

The old-style skateboard has been overtaken by a trio of new deals-on-wheels. Take the Micro Skate Scooter. It's a compact, manually powered chrome machine used by fashionable urban types to get around town.

"I was given mine for my 26th birthday," explains PR consultant[1] Nikki Roberts. "I thought my boyfriend was joking at first. Now I'm totally converted. It's great for cardiovascular workout[2] and looks really cool. You do get looks of amazement and the odd request to have a go, but that's OK."

Then there's the mountain board. Used to train on during the summer by the British Olympic Snowboarding team, skateboarders have now begun to adopt the board as one of their own. "It's one of the best ways to get round London – you just cruise over every kerb and uneven surface," says Declan McEnery, a recent convert. "It's like carving in fresh powder snow. It doesn't slip or slide on wet surfaces and your feet are held in place, so you can do a lot more moves than on a normal skateboard. And you can get up to 40mph in hilly areas."

Bicycles come in all shapes and sizes, but currently the most loved is the Raleigh Chopper; the classic 'Easy Rider' bikes for Seventies kids. Now a collector's item – DJ Norman Jay is the proud owner of a set– the sight of this retro-joy-toy brings memories flooding back for spectators and riders. "It makes me feel young again," explains IT consultant Richard Westen, 37. "People always stop and stare – that's half the rush."

Shelley Fannell

1   PR Consultant: someone who specialises in 'public relations' – the links that a company has with the general public
2   Cardiovascular workout: exercises for the heart

- Why does the writer think these new ways of getting around town are now becoming popular?
- What reaction does Nikki Roberts get when she rides her Micro Skate Scooter?
- Which bicycle brings back memories of the 1970s?

4 Language skills

Word

Shelley Fannell's article is written in a very lively style. She has chosen words which catch the reader's attention and match the modern, up-to-date subject she is writing about. Read through the article again and look out for alliteration, rhyme, hyphenated word-groups and words which are fairly new to the language.

Alliteration is the repetition of consonant sounds to achieve a particular effect.

A good example of alliteration in this review is: *funky, fun and foot-powered*, where the repeated *f* sounds make the phrase stand out.

1 Advertisers have always loved alliteration: think about *Pick up a Penguin*. In pairs, jot down as many advertising slogans as you can which use alliteration. Pick out your favourite and explain how the alliteration helps to make the slogan memorable.

2 Use alliteration to create some slogans of your own to advertise:

- a new chocolate bar
- a range of shoes
- instant meals
- any new product of your own choice

Words which end with the same (or similar) sounds are said to **rhyme**.

Look back at the second paragraph of the review to see how the writer uses the phrase *deals-on-wheels*. It is effective because:

- the rhyme *deals–wheels* makes the phrase stand out
- it neatly gets across the idea that this is good-value transport (***good*** deals)
- it jokingly reminds you of the phrase *meals-on-wheels* – something which is for the old, whereas this transport is for the young

Advertisers seem to like rhyme as much as alliteration. For example, when the railways wanted to get across the idea that rail travel is less stressful than driving, they came up with the slogan *Let the train take the strain*.

3 What ideas or points are the advertisers trying to convey with these rhyming slogans? Write an explanation for each one.

- *A Mars a day helps you work rest and play*
- *Great Little Rooster Booster* (eggs)
- *Beanz Meanz Heinz*

Spelling

1 The article contains some common prefixes: *micro-*, *bi-* and *spect-*. Use a dictionary to check what each one means. Write down some other examples of words which contain each of these prefixes, paying special attention to the spellings. Next to each word, note down its meaning.

Sentence

Speech marks (" ") are used to mark the beginning and end of someone's actual words when they are quoted in a piece of writing. Speech marks are also called inverted commas or quotation marks. They can be written as single inverted commas (' ') or as doubles (" ").

The 'New deals on wheels' article uses double inverted commas for speech.

1 To make sure that you know the main rules for punctuating speech, look back at the article and write down the rules for:

- where you open and close the speech marks
- whether you end a speech with a full stop or a comma

Text

The structure of a text is the way it is put together in paragraphs.

1 Look back to Unit 3 (pages 20–25) to remind yourself about paragraphs. Then write a topic heading for each of the paragraphs in the 'New deals on wheels' article.

2 Shelley Fannell, the writer of this article, has chosen to round it off with someone's comment on riding the Raleigh Chopper. Draft a brief paragraph which could be added at the end as a conclusion, to sum up the main points or draw everything together. You could pick up some ideas from the introduction.

5 ▶ Planning your own writing

Write your own article in which you review a range of new products or facilities.

▶▶ STARTING POINTS

You could choose to survey products such as footwear, clothing or computer games; or you could give your comments on the range of sports facilities or the variety of clubs in your area.

▶▶ CLUES FOR SUCCESS

- Choose a range of products or facilities that you are interested in and have used yourself.

- Plan a clear structure.

- Write your article in an up-to-date way to suit the subject you have chosen.

- Use alliteration and rhyming phrases to capture the reader's interest.

- Include quotes from people who have used the products or facilities.

▶▶ REDRAFTING AND IMPROVING

Look carefully at your first draft. Check that you have:

- produced a clear structure which makes the article easy to read and understand

- expressed your comments clearly

- written in a lively and entertaining way

- included correctly punctuated quotes

>> WRITING FRAME

To give you some ideas, here is a writing frame for an article which reviews local cinemas.

Local cinema review

Paragraph and structure	Content	Possible opening phrases
1 Introduction	• why more cinemas have been built in recent years • the popularity of films • different types of cinema	*As people are getting tired of sitting at home with a video...*
2 Small, local, old-fashioned cinemas	• why some people prefer them • what they offer which is different or 'alternative'	*The old-style flea-pit has had a new lease of life...* *"I'm a regular," says...*
3 Big local cinemas	• less successful than they were	*Then there's the Odeon...*
4 Multiplexes	• their advantages • why they are growing	*Cinemas come in all shapes and sizes...* *"I'm totally converted..."*
5 Conclusion	• what's the future for these three types?	*When you look at what these different cinemas have to offer...*

6 ▷ Looking back

- **Alliteration** and **rhyme** are some of the language features which can help your writing seem lively and up-to-date.

- **Speech marks** are used to mark off the beginning and the end of someone's words when they are quoted in writing. It is important to follow all the rules about punctuating speech if you want your writing to be understood.

- Articles and essays need a clear **structure**. This should be planned before you start your first draft.

Blockbuster

1 ▷ Purpose

In this unit you will:

- read a news item on the film *Chicken Run*
- learn about the kind of language that people use when they are commenting on films
- write your own news item in which you comment on a new film or television series

▶▶ **Subject links:** *art, media studies*

2 ▷ Commenting on a new film

This article appeared on the Online News site, a few days before the film Chicken Run *opened in the United States.*

| Back | Forward | Home | Reload | Images | Print | Find | Stop |

Location: http://onlinenews.co.uk

| What's New? | What's Cool? | Handbook | Net Search | Net Directory | |

Front Page | World | UK | UK Politics | Business | Sci/Tech | Health | Education | Sport | Entertainment |
Talking Point | High Graphics | AudioVideo | Feedback | Help | Noticias | Newyddion |

Entertainment Contents: New Music Releases |

Online News: Entertainment

Friday, 23 June, 2000, 10:48 GMT 11:48

UK *Chicken Run* sets US flapping

Cinema box offices across the US are gearing up for an extra busy weekend with the much-anticipated opening of *Chicken Run* – the first feature-length movie from the makers of Wallace and Gromit.

Nick Park and Peter Lord are the brains and talent behind the award-winning British clay animation company Aardman.

After the huge global success of their three Wallace and Gromit shorts, *Chicken Run* has already won a string of rave reviews in the week leading up to its US release.

At the Hollywood première this week, Lord and Park were given the full red-carpet treatment, with the paparazzi[1] amassed around them and flash bulbs popping.

Based on the 1963 Steve McQueen movie *The Great Escape*, *Chicken Run* tells of the desperate attempts of a group of hens to escape from the cruel regime of Tweedy's egg farm.

Hollywood actor Mel Gibson and British actresses Julia Sawalha, Jane Horrocks and Miranda Richardson are among those voicing the movie.

[1] paparazzi: *newspaper photographers who follow celebrities around*

44

But, as with *The Wrong Trousers* and *A Close Shave*, it is Lord and Park's imaginative and humorous plasticine creations who are the real stars of the film.

'Spectacular'

In the run-up to this weekend, *The New York Post* hailed *Chicken Run* as 'a triumph' and 'the wittiest and best voiced animation film to come along in years'.

USA Today described it as 'a classic for the ages', adding: '*Chicken Run* boasts the most-delicious collection of desperately funny Brits since *The Full Monty*.'

Rolling Stone called it 'spectacular', while *Good Morning America*, *US Weekly* and *The Today Show* saw it as the funniest film so far this year.

Chicken Run marks the first product of a five-film collaboration between Bristol-based Aardman and Steven Spielberg's DreamWorks studio.

The painstaking work on the project took four years to complete. During this time, DreamWorks stayed away from the Aardman warehouses to let Park and Lord get on with making the kind of film they wanted.

Accent

Freedom to experiment was the main reason that Park and Lord had not attempted to make a full-length film before. After Wallace and Gromit, and their series of Creature Comforts spots, the duo had been offered countless books and screenplays to adapt. But they couldn't find the right project that would be distinctly theirs – until they were approached by Spielberg's company.

DreamWorks simply said it wanted to make a prison-of-war escape movie with chickens. Spielberg himself owns hundreds of chickens and is a big fan of the McQueen classic.

Ultimately, say Park and Lord, it was the sheer simplicity of the idea that gave it its appeal.

The only drawback to *Chicken Run* – as far as US audiences are concerned – is one also encountered by Wallace and Gromit: suggestions that people will not understand the chickens' northern English accents.

Some Hollywood producers say the film should be given an American voiceover.

However, Aardman has resisted, instead simply agreeing to provide audiences with printed translations for words such as 'codswallop', if required.

Chicken Run opens in the UK on 30 June.

3 ❯ Key features

The writer:
- uses wordplay in the headline to catch the reader's attention
- quotes reviews of *Chicken Run* from newspapers and magazines
- arranges all the different points in a very clear structure

- What are the names of the two British animators who have made *Chicken Run*? How long did the film take to complete?
- Who owns the DreamWorks studio in America?
- What difficulty might American audiences have with the film?

4 Language skills

Word

Wordplay is the name given to the games that people play with words in order to achieve a special effect. Wordplay is usually humorous, but not always.

Headline writers will often use wordplay to get a humorous effect and capture the reader's attention.

1 To understand the wordplay in the headline of the *Chicken Run* article, you have to be aware of the two meanings of *flapping*. What are they?

2 Write explanations of the wordplay in these headlines:

* *Cat-flap in Downing Street* (above a story about Humphrey, the Prime Minister's cat, who had gone missing)

* *There's no place like gnome* (a report about a man who had complained about all the plastic gnomes in his neighbour's garden)

* *Too wet to woo* (owls in a local zoo were not mating because of the damp conditions)

* *Who's a twitty boy?* (a boy had to be saved by firemen after he had climbed a tree to rescue his parrot)

* *Golfer is beaten black and roo* (Australian golfer was attacked by a kangaroo)

Spelling

In the article you will find a comment about the 'humorous plasticine creations' of Nick Park and Peter Lord. Notice the difference between the spelling of the adjective *humorous* and the noun *humour*.

1 Write down the words ending in *-our* which mean:

* a person who lives next door

* work

* a kind or helpful act

* red, green, blue, yellow, etc...

Sentence

Quotation marks (" ") – also known as inverted commas or speech marks – are used to show that a word or phrase is quoted from somewhere else. They can be written as single inverted commas (' ') or double inverted commas (" ") and are also used in the punctuation of speech.

In this article, quotation marks have been placed around *a triumph* because they were the exact words used in the *New York Post*.

1 Here are some **quotes** from reviews on *Chicken Run*, with the names of the magazines and Web sites they come from written in brackets. Complete the article '*Chickens send their rivals running*' which follows them, adding the quotes in the right places.

smart and charming
(*culturevulture.net*)

a family film in the best sense
(*culturevulture.net*)

a delightful tale (*eonline.com*)

by far the single smartest family
animation feature I have seen
(*filmcritic.com*)

highly enjoyable
(*goodauthority.org*)

every moment is rich with detail
and movement (*roughcut.com*)

near perfection (*USA Today*)

delightfully clever (*Variety*)

Text

Structure is the name given to the way a writer has organised a text into sections, in order to make it easy to follow and interesting to read.

❶ The *Chicken Run* article can be divided into six main sections, listed below. Reread it carefully and decide where each section begins. Jot down the opening phrase of each sentence.

Section

1 the introduction: *Chicken Run*'s successful opening in America

2 what the film is about

3 the actors doing the voices and the characters in the story

4 the reviews

5 the background: how the project came about

6 a special feature of the film: the northern English accents

Chickens send their rivals running

Nick Park's *Chicken Run* has taken America by storm. **eonline.com** set the pattern by calling it _____. And, while **filmcritic.com** declared the film to be _____, the **culturevulture.net** reviewer described it as _____ and _____.

roughcut.com was enthusiastic about the animation, adding _____, a comment echoed by the critics of *USA Today* (_____) and *Variety* (_____). For the movie Web site **goodauthority.org**, and for the audiences who will be viewing it over the coming weeks, it was simply _____.

47

5 ▸ Planning your own writing

Write your own online news article, commenting on a new film or television series.

▶▶ STARTING POINT

Choose a film or television series which you have seen and which has just been reviewed in newspapers, magazines and on Web sites. You can find short review quotes on sites such as *movies.yahoo.com* (simply enter the name of the film that you are interested in, and, when the home-page appears, click on *reviews*).

▶▶ CLUES FOR SUCCESS

Make sure that your writing really reads like an online news article:

- use wordplay in the headline to attract the reader's attention
- include quotes (remembering to punctuate them correctly)
- work out a clear structure before you start

▶▶ REDRAFTING AND IMPROVING

Check that you have:

- written in a style which sounds like a news article
- created a clear structure
- included quotes and punctuated them correctly

6 ▸ Looking back

- News articles which comment on new films are usually a mixture of facts and **quotes**.
- When people write headlines, they try to make them eye-catching; often they will use **wordplay**.
- It is important to plan a clear **structure**; this makes the writing easier to understand and more interesting.

>> WRITING FRAME

This writing frame will give you a possible structure
and some ideas for opening phrases.

An article on a new film or television series

Paragraph and content	Opening phrases
Headline	
1 Introduction	*Last week saw the London premiere of...*
2 What it's about	*Based on a true story about...*
3 The main actors	*Hollywood actress XX plays the central role of Y... , with support from British favourite AA, fresh from his appearance in B...*
4 The reviews	*The reviews have been amazing. The Daily Mirror called it '_____', while the critic of the movie Web site eonline.com declared it '_____' ...*
5 The background: how the film came to be made; who had the idea; which people came together to get the project going...	*Work on this project took four years to complete...* *What really appealed to director XX was...*
6 A special feature	*One problem has been... (or)* *One of the most enjoyable things has been...*
7 Conclusion	*As director XX said, '_____'...*

I wish to make a complaint...

1 ❯ Purpose

In this unit you will:
- read a letter of complaint
- learn about the kind of language that people use when they are writing complaint letters
- write your own letter in which you make comments

❯❯ **Subject link:** *PSHE*

2 ❯ Commenting through letters

Stripped-off

This letter was written to a well-known football club by a parent of an eleven-year-old boy.

3 ❯ Key°features

The writer:
- varies his vocabulary to avoid repetition
- clearly explains the order in which things happened
- uses the correct format for a formal letter

❯❯
- How would you summarise James Burrows' complaint in one sentence?
- What is the latest thing to have happened at the football club, to make him angry?
- In his concluding paragraph, what is he asking the Director of Marketing to do?

19 Maine Close
Stretford
Lancashire
MM1 0FC

April 2nd, 2001

JB Carlton
Director of Marketing
Barchester United Football Club
Lancashire
MM10 1FA

Dear Mr Carlton,

Last Christmas I purchased a complete United kit for my son. Within
a fortnight you had brought out a new away strip. By March you were
advertising yet another outfit specially designed for your appearance in
the Cup Final. At last week's home game I read in your programme that
you have changed your kit manufacturers and will be bringing out a
completely new strip next season. Now I hear on the news that Dean
Barton is to be transferred, which means that my son's number 13 shirt
with the player's name on the back will be out of date.

You must be aware that young supporters want to be seen in the latest
team shirt and put pressure on their parents to buy every new strip that
comes out. Fashion is important to young people: they don't like to be
seen in out-of-date clothes. So they ask for new strips at birthdays and
Christmas or save up their pocket money to buy them.

Your club must be making a fortune out of supporters in this way. Some
people might say that you are exploiting them.

I am hoping that you will explain to me how you are planning to ensure
that loyal fans are not going to be ripped off in future.

Yours sincerely,

James Burrows

James Burrows

4 ▷ Language skills

Word

A **synonym** is a word which means the same, or almost the same, as another word.

Synonyms are useful when you want to avoid repeating yourself, as James Burrows found in his letter.

❶ Because his complaint was about his team's shirt, shorts and socks, he had to refer to them several times. To avoid repeating the same word, he used three synonyms in the first three sentences. What are they?

❷ Find synonyms for the words highlighted in the following sentences and phrases. They are all useful in letter-writing. To start you off, a possible example has been given for the first one

- *I want to **say** this very clearly. (state)*

- *I hope to **get** an **answer** from you within the next month.*

- *I **bought** a new set last week.*

- *It is my **view** that...*

- *The service was **very bad**.*

Spelling

An **antonym** is a word which has the opposite meaning to another word. The term comes from *anti-*, a prefix which means *against*. Many antonyms are formed by adding a **negative prefix**.

Look back to Unit 1 (page 10) to remind yourself about negative prefixes. The rule is that, when you add a negative prefix, you do not change the spelling of the root word. For example, when *appear* becomes *disappear*, it is still spelt with one *s* and two *p*s.

❶ Here are six negative prefixes: *un-, ir-, in-, dis-, im-, il-*. Which one is usually added to each of these six words? Match them up, write them down and check the spellings.

> *agree, convenient, legible, relevant, polite, known*

Sentence

Time adverbials are words and phrases which tell you *when* something happened.

They are especially useful when you are describing a sequence of events. For example, you might want to say:

Afterwards, I found that...
*We **then** took it to be repaired...*
***Three weeks later** I received a letter...*
***Since that time** I have not heard...*
*I am **now** considering...*
***In future** I will avoid...*

❶ Find the five time adverbials used in the first paragraph of the letter.

❷ Draw a time-line of the period covered in the letter: December to April. Use the information provided by the time adverbials to place on the time-line the five events which have caused James Burrows to write his letter.

Text

Personal letters are ones we send to our friends or members of the family. **Formal letters** have to be business-like and are often sent to people we hardly know or do not know at all.

❶ Here are the openings to some letters. Decide whether each one is from a personal letter or a formal letter.

Dear Uncle Jim,
Thank you for my birthday present...

Dear Ms Brown,
Your check-up is now due...

Hi, Lucy!
Just letting you know...

Dear Sir,
This is to inform you that...

Mary –
A quick note to say...

Dear all,
Having a great time...

5 Planning your own writing

Write a formal letter of complaint.

- Synonyms will help you to avoid repeating key words too often.

- Make sure that you follow the conventions for formal letter writing. Use the letter on page 51 as an example of how a formal letter ought to be set out.

▶▶ **REDRAFTING AND IMPROVING**

Reread your letter. Check that you have:

- made the point of your complaint very clear

- explained exactly what the problem is

- asked for some action to be taken

- used synonyms to avoid repeating key words

- followed the conventions for layout

▶▶ **STARTING POINTS**

You could complain about:

- bad service (you always have to wait for ages to be served, or the buses never come on time...)

- faulty goods (a tee-shirt shrank the first time you washed it, or your computer keeps crashing...)

- poor facilities in your local area (there aren't enough things for young people to do, or there's no swimming pool within miles...)

- an unfair situation (the school rules need to be changed, or age-limits are too low...)

 **WRITING FRAME**

Here is a writing frame which offers you some ideas about how to structure your letter and gives some examples of phrases you might use.

A formal letter

Paragraph and contents	Language features	Useful phrases
1 Introduce the subject	synonyms	*I wish to complain about...* *I am writing to you about...* *I would welcome your comments on...*
2 Explain the problem	time adverbials	*This is the sequence of events...* *The next thing that happened was...* *In future...*
3 Make a criticism	negative prefixes	*This is unacceptable...* *I do not agree with...* *I refuse to accept that...*
4 Suggest a solution or make a request		*May I suggest that...* *I should be grateful if...* *I should like to know whether...* *Perhaps you could let me know...*

6 ▷ Looking back

- A **synonym** is a word which means the same, or almost the same as another word. Synonyms add variety to your writing, and are useful when you want to avoid repeating key words.

- **Time adverbials** tell the reader when events happened.

- **Formal letters** are ones written to people you hardly know or have not met at all. They are business-like and there are certain conventions which you have to follow when setting them out. Letters written to friends and family are called personal letters.

In the commentary box

1 **Purpose**

In this unit you will:

- read some comments about a famous sportsperson
- learn about some of the language that sports writers use
- write your own commentary on figures from the world of sport or entertainment

➤➤ **Subject links:** *sport, music, PSHE*

2 **Newspaper comments and judgements**

Sportsperson of the twentieth century

At the end of the twentieth century, newspapers were full of articles on the Band of the Century or the Greatest Political Leader of the Century. Shakespeare was even voted Man of the Millennium! Here are some newspaper comments on the sportsperson of the twentieth century, collected together in an article in the Guardian newspaper.

Ali is proclaimed the greatest

As the last week of the twentieth century drew to a close, newspapers around the world published the results of their polls for sportsperson of the last 100 years. Almost without exception, one man received the bulk of the votes – Muhammed Ali.

The *Independent* attempted to explain his legend: 'Ali was more than just a boxer. Of the 99 other distinguished names on our list, perhaps only Pele, the runner-up, could make the beginnings of a similar claim... But, in truth, he and the other 98 belong to the world of sport. Muhammed Ali belongs to the world.'

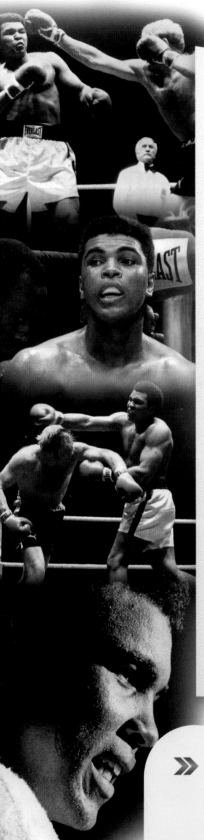

Adam Parsons in the *Sunday Business* said that a mixture of things had kept us in love with Ali: '...the single reason why his legend lives on is that in one person we find qualities to satisfy every sports fan – the technical skill of a great boxer, the looks of a model... the mind of a deep-thinker and the reflex wit of a stand-up comedian.'

In other countries the praise was just as great. Gavin Evans wrote in South Africa's *Mail and Guardian*: 'He was the first global sports star – for over a decade or so the world's most famous person – and through his use of this position he opened the way for the Michael Jordans and Tiger Woods of today.'

In his home country, *USA Today*'s Jon Saraceno said that Ali was the ultimate sporting superstar: 'No one had the worldwide impact of Ali. His popularity over four decades is unrivaled... I like to think of him as the best example of the "A Package": athleticism, artistry, accomplishment, alpha-star appeal and ambassadorship[1]. He stood for something besides himself.'

Adapted from 'The Editor', The Guardian, *31 December 1999*

[1] ambassadorship: *a respected representative for his country, sport and people*

3 Key features

The writer:
- includes examples of exaggeration
- uses quotations from other journalists
- gives a survey of people's opinions

» • Who came first and second in the polls for sportsperson of the century?
- Which sports were they famous for?
- Which four personal qualities of the sportsperson of the century does Adam Parsons list in the third paragraph?

4 ▸ Language skills

Word

As you learned in Unit 1 (page 10), **abstract nouns** are the labels we give to things we cannot touch, see or hear, such as emotions, feelings or ideas.

It is almost impossible to write about a person's qualities without using abstract nouns.

1 See how many abstract nouns you can pick out of the article. List the ones which label Ali's qualities, as the writers see them.

Alliteration is the repetition of consonant sounds to achieve a particular effect.

Sports writers like to use alliteration. For example, because Ali was witty and talkative, he was known as the *Louisville Lip*.

2 Which phrase uses alliteration to draw together five of Ali's qualities?

Spelling

Sportsperson is an example of a **compound word**: a word made up of two or more other words – in this case, *sports* and *person*. Many of our commonest words are compounds, such as *teapot* (*tea+pot*) or *blackbird* (*black+bird*).

If a compound word looks confusing when it is written down, it is written with a **hyphen**, as with *breast-stroke* and *co-worker*. The simple spelling rule is that, when you put two words together to make a compound word, you do not normally change the spelling of either word.

1 Put words from List a together with words from List b to form compounds. If they look confusing, they will need hyphens.

List a: *rattle, bus, arm, water, life, light, pick, out, foot*

List b: *fall, pocket, ball, driver, chair, house, time, look, snake.*

Sentence

The **colon** (:) is a punctuation mark which shows that there is something else to follow in the sentence.

In the article on Muhammed Ali, the colon is used to introduce lists and quotations.

1 Find the colon used to introduce a list towards the end of the article.

2 Find the four uses of the colon to introduce quotations.

Hyperbole is the name given to exaggeration in writing or speech. (Pronounce it 'high–purr–berley', with the stress on the second syllable.)

Writers often use hyperbole when they want to make a very exaggerated statement about somebody: they might want to build them up as the greatest or fastest or funniest. For example, a film critic might write: 'On his day, nobody is funnier than Jim Carrey.' Many people might disagree; but the writer really just wants to express a strong opinion, and the hyperbole helps her to do it.

3 Look at these statements from the article. Decide whether each one is a statement of fact that nobody could argue with, or purely the writer's opinion, expressed through hyperbole.

Pele… and the other 98 belong to the world of sport. Muhammed Ali belongs to the world.

He was the first global sports star…

…for over a decade or so the world's most famous person…

Text

An article like this one, which contains examples of a range of opinions, is called a **survey**. The writer quotes from a number of **sources**: places where information and opinions can be found.

1 How many sources are quoted in this article?

2 If you are writing about 'the best' in a particular field, you will probably want to compare your chosen person with other people. An article on the world's best footballer will refer to others who might rival him for the title, as well as to footballers who have been influenced by him.

Which one man rivalled Ali as sportsperson of the century?

3 Which two men are named as having owed some of their success to Ali? Which sports do they play? How did Ali's achievements help them?

5 ▷ Planning your own writing

Write your own article on 'The Best (person) of the decade'.

▷▷ STARTING POINTS

- You might find it most enjoyable to survey the world of sport or entertainment. For example, you could write about the best band, singer, film actor, footballer or stand-up comedian.

- You could write about an individual, a group or a team.

▷▷ CLUES FOR SUCCESS

- Use the Internet to research the different people in whichever field you choose. For example, every football club and rock band has its own Web site; and there are a number of sites where you can find out about films and film actors.

- Collect quotations about your subject from as many different sources as you can. For example, the Web site of a band will have pages where you can find reviews of their latest album.

- When you write your article, make it a survey of people's opinions, like the one on Muhammed Ali. Say where the quotations come from, and link them with your own comments.

- Some of the 'best' comments will contain hyperbole.

▷▷ REDRAFTING AND IMPROVING

Look back through your survey. Check that you have:

- written a clear introduction
- introduced each of the sources
- used a colon before each quotation

WRITING FRAME

This writing frame is for an article called 'The best young goal-scorer of the past five years: Michael Owen'.

The best young goal-scorer of the past five years: Michael Owen

Paragraph and content	Sources (where you can find the quotations)	Possible opening phrases/ quotations from source
1 Introduction • say who are you writing about: Michael Owen • summarise what the sources have generally said about him		
2 Start the survey • introduce the first source • quote from the source	A book: *Shoot Annual 2000*	*Shoot Annual 2000* highlighted Owen's value... 'Liverpool were allegedly offered £25 million by Lazio for the striker, while he became the star every football-mad youngster wants to be...'
3 • introduce the second source • quote from it	Official Liverpool FC Web site: www.liverpoolfc.net	The Official Liverpool FC Web site's list of Owen's achievements backs up this opinion... 'He is the youngest player to play for England...'
4, 5, 6 Introduce other sources and quote from them	Other books, magazines and newspapers Other Web sites	In an article from Match of the Day magazine...
7 Conclusion • identify the major qualities which make him 'the best'		

---

6 Looking back

- Writers choose their vocabulary very carefully when they are describing a person's qualities; these qualities will be labelled by **abstract nouns**.

- The **colon** can be use to introduce a list or a quotation.

- Exaggeration in writing or speech is called **hyperbole**. Writers use it to express strong opinions.

- An article about a number of different people's views is called a **survey**. The newspapers, books and Web sites which provide information for your research are known as **sources**.

From different angles

1 ⟩ **Purpose**

In this unit you will:

- read three different extracts on the same subject
- think about the different kinds of writing: writing to analyse, to review and to comment
- write three different pieces of your own, analysing, reviewing and commenting on the same subject

⟫ **Subject links:** *history, art*

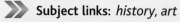

www.cine-online.com/moviezone/guides/gladia

w? | What's Cool? | Handbook | Net Search

2 ⟩ **Commenting on a new film**

Gladiator

Gladiator is a major epic film set in ancient Rome, featuring fierce battles, huge crowd scenes and terrifying fights with tigers.

WRITING TO ANALYSE

The first of these extracts is a brief analysis of the film taken from an online movie guide.

GLADIATOR

Starring Joaquin Phoenix, Connie Nielsen & Russell Crowe

Oscar for Best Picture   Oscar for Best Actor   Oscar for Best Costume

*The epic story of a man who dared
to challenge the power of ancient Rome*

Not since the heady days of *Ben Hur* and *Spartacus* have movie screens seen an epic of these dimensions. Now director Ridley Scott takes you back into the violent world of the Roman gladiator in a dramatic tale of love, heroism and bloody revenge.

When the great General Maximus (Russell Crowe) makes his triumphant return after yet another victory, he looks forward to a quiet retirement with his wife and son. But his hopes are to be dramatically dashed; the dying Emperor Marcus Aurelius (Richard Harris) imposes one more duty upon him – to succeed as Emperor.

Furious at being set aside, and bitterly jealous of Maximus's success, the heir to the throne, Commodus (Joaquin Phoenix), has Maximus's wife and son brutally murdered. Maximus himself is forced into slavery where his fame quickly grows as one of Rome's most skilful and deadly gladiators.

Realising that his only chance of gaining revenge is to win over the Roman people, Maximus sets about becoming the greatest gladiator the crowds have ever seen...

- Who is the director of *Gladiator*?
- Who is its star and what character does he play?
- Which power, stronger than the emperor's, does he hope to get on his side?

WRITING TO REVIEW

As soon as a film comes out, hundreds of reviews appear in newspapers and magazines, and they can all be found on the Internet. A Web site like Yahoo! Movies (movies.yahoo.com) will give you a selection of review extracts. This is the selection that appeared about Gladiator.

Yahoo! Movies: Gladiator (2000) Reviews

Back | Forward | Home | Reload | Images | Print | Find | Stop

Location: http://movies.yahoo.com

What's New? | What's Cool? | Handbook | Net Search | Net Directory

24 Frames Per Second:
'Ridley Scott's Gladiator is a movie for boys.'

Nzone:
'Gladiator is terrific, awe-inspiring story-telling on all levels, and is sure to have viewers rooting along with the crowds in the film.'

Days of Thunder:
'Gladiator is a film of two minds. It wants desperately to be taken seriously and shows it through its somber tone…'

Flick Filosopher:
Is Gladiator an action-movie? Is it an historical drama? Is it a sweeping epic? Yes.'

Harvey's Movie Reviews:
'Spellbinding historical drama from director Ridley Scott…'

James Berardinelli:
'This is film-making on a grand scale.'

JoBlo's Movie Emporium:
'A sprawling epic set ablaze by massive sets, genuine authenticity, awesome battle sequences and a good ol'fashioned story dipped in power, love and revenge.'

Los Angeles Times:
'Russell Crowe's muscular performance, stylish battle scenes and rich atmosphere help to cut through the shortcomings…'

Movie Bodega:
'Skewering history for the good parts and throwing out the facts, Gladiator is the thinking-man's summer movie… a bubbly tale of heroism and virtue with enough violence to shame the most ardent Mel Gibson fan.'

Movie Juice!:
'Russell Crowe is the real star here and he shines supernova bright.'

Orlando Weekly Movies:
'Special effects in movies have become increasingly wedded to science-fiction, but in the glorious spectacle Gladiator, director Ridley Scott uses this technology to re-create the Roman Empire that once blanketed most of Europe.'

Pop Matters:
'Derek Jacobi… plays an outspoken senator in a manner that's so wooden you might think he was auditioning for The Phantom Menace.'

Variety:
'A muscular and bloody combat picture, a compelling revenge drama and a truly transporting trip back nearly 2,000 years, Ridley Scott's bold epic of imperial intrigue and heroism brings new luster and excitement to a tarnished genre…'

- According to *Flick Filosopher, Gladiator* is three types of movie in one. Which three types?
- Which strong qualities make up for the film's weaknesses, according to the *Los Angeles Times*?
- Which actor is criticised for his bad acting in one review?

WRITING TO COMMENT

The director of Gladiator, *Ridley Scott, was interviewed for an online movie news programme. He was asked whether Russell Crowe (who plays the hero) was scared when he filmed the scenes in the arena with the tigers. This is how he replied.*

Location:

| What's New? | What's Cool? | Handbook | Net Search | Net Directory | |

No, he's not frightened of anything. The thing with those tigers is that they won't do as they're told. They're basically about eleven feet from the tip of their tail to the tip of their nose, and they're about six hundred pounds, and they'll move about as fast as your cat. So the worst thing about them is that, when you say, 'Action!', they'll never follow through on what they've been trained to do. They tend to wander about and scratch themselves… so that becomes the downside to working with Bengal tigers.

Then occasionally the Bengal would be running right here, right here at the end of the chain, and there's no bars, and four guys are standing there all the time with a big metal ring attached to the ground in big wooden sleepers. Those four guys are there all the time keeping an eye on the tigers.

Suddenly it'd be on its feet and the whole camera crew would scramble, and there'd be four cameras left like little islands unmanned, because… it'd give a big loud roar and it would remind us of what they could actually do.

3 Key features

- The writers of the analytical article are aiming to explain what kind of film it is. They set the background and give a summary.

- The writers of the reviews often use simile and metaphor to express their ideas vividly.

- Ridley Scott is giving a comment about the film and his star. He gives his impression of things that happened while making the film.

- How long are the tigers, and how much do they weigh?
- What is the main difficulty when you try to film them?
- Whose job was it to look after the tigers? How would they try to control them?

65

4 > Language skills

Word

A **simile** is a way of comparing things, often in an unusual or unexpected way, in which the writer creates an image in the reader's mind. A simile uses the words *like* or *as*.

1 Write down the simile Ridley Scott uses to describe what the cameras looked like after they had been deserted by the frightened crew. He says that they were...

Metaphor is a way of comparing things without using the words *like* or *as*.

2 Write down the metaphor one reviewer on page 64 uses to follow up the idea that Russell Crowe is the star of the film.

Personification is a special kind of metaphor in which things and ideas are spoken about as though they were people or other living creatures.

We use a lot of personification in everyday speech. We talk about *Mother Nature* and *Father Time*; we say that the Sun *has hidden itself* behind a cloud; or that *life can play some nasty tricks*.

3 Which review extract on page 64 asks us to think of the film *Gladiator* as someone who can't decide what sort of person they want to be?

Spelling

One of the review extracts on page 64 contains the word *somber*, which means dark and gloomy. This is the American spelling: in British English we write *sombre*. Most words are spelt the same in American English (AE) and British English (BE) but you will come across some differences when you read American texts (and many people who speak other languages use American spellings when they write English too).

1 This is how a number of words are spelt in American English. What are their British spellings?

catalog, center, check (that you get from a bank), *color, honor, humor, theater, traveling, jewelry, pajamas, plow, defense, offense, pretense, tire* (on a wheel)

2 Find the other American English spelling in the final review extract. How would we spell it in British English? Compare it with *somber*, *center* and *theater*. Then make up a rule for words ending with these letters in AE and BE.

Sentence

The **semicolon** (;) is a punctuation mark which can be used to join two main clauses in a sentence.

We often want to write two statements about the same subject. For example:

> I loved Gladiator. *It was exciting to watch.*

When the second statement seems to follow on from the first, it can be joined on with a semicolon:

> I loved Gladiator; *it was exciting to watch.*

The semicolon shows that the two clauses are connected in meaning. The writer in the online movie guide (page 63) uses the semicolon in this way in his second paragraph because his two statements are connected in meaning.

1 Which pairs of sentences below could be joined by a semicolon, and which could not? Explain your decision in each case.

- *Maximus dreams of home.*
- *He wants only to return to his wife and family.*

- *The old Emperor was dying.*
- *The Roman people loved games and circuses.*

- *Maximus is forced to train as a gladiator.*
- *This is where his fame grows.*

Text

Different kinds of films (such as horror movies, Westerns, war films and science-fiction films) are called **genres**. It is a French word and has a French pronunciation.

One of the reviewers on page 64 writes: 'Is *Gladiator* an action movie? Is it an historical drama? Is it a sweeping epic?' The question is immediately answered – 'Yes' – meaning that it belongs to all three of these film genres:

- action movie – a film which includes a great deal of exciting action, such as car chases and gun-fights

- historical drama – a film set in an earlier historical period

- epic – a spectacular film which includes dramatic and heroic events covering many years

1 James Bond films are examples of action movies. Write down some titles of films which belong to these genres: *war, science-fiction, Western, fantasy, horror.*

2 One of the other reviewers calls *Gladiator* a 'combat picture' and a 'revenge drama'. Write down what you think each of these terms means. Then try to think of examples of other films which could fit into those two genres.

5 ▷ Planning your own writing

Write three short pieces based on either a new film or a new television soap (it could be real, or one you have invented). The first piece should be an analysis. The second piece of writing should be a review article, or set of review quotations. The third should be someone's comments.

⟫ STARTING POINTS

First, look back at the examples of writing to analyse, review and comment on *Gladiator*, at the beginning of this unit. Then decide whether you are going to write about a new TV soap or a new film.

Writing about a new TV soap

If you decide to base your writing on a new soap:

- your *analysis* could be an article in a TV magazine describing where the soap is going to be set, what characters will be in it, what the main storylines might be

- you could then write a collection of short *review* comments which appeared in the newspapers the day after the first episode (like those on page 64), or a single review from a newspaper, magazine or Web site of your choice

- a final *comment* piece could be an article on soaps generally: Are they mindless rubbish or harmless fun? Do we need another one? Does this new soap provide anything new and original?

Writing about a new film

If you decide to base your writing on a new film:

- Your *analysis* could be one from a Web site page like the one on page 63.

- You could either write a single *review*, or a collection of review extracts like those on page 64.

- Choose one aspect of the film to write a *comment* on. For example, it could be the designer's comments on the special effects or the director's comments on working with animals and children.

⟫ CLUES FOR SUCCESS

- Think about using simile, metaphor and personification – they can help you to express your ideas vividly.

- Remember how useful the semicolon can be for joining two related statements together.

- Compare your film or soap with others in the genre. If it's a soap, how different is it from *Brookside*, *Coronation Street* or *Eastenders*?

⟫ REDRAFTING AND IMPROVING

In groups or pairs, look closely at your own and other people's first attempts.

- Make suggestions for improving, editing or adding more detail.

- Is the language interesting? Have your review quotations used vivid and original similes and metaphors, for example? Have you talked about genre?

 WRITING FRAMES

This is how you could structure an article to analyse a new television soap.

Analyse: a TV magazine article on a new television soap

Paragraph and structure	Content
1 Introduction	• the soap's title • when it will be shown • where it will be set
2, 3 The story	• examples of storylines
4, 5 The cast	• well-known actors — what they have played in the past — and the roles they will be playing in the soap • new, young actors
6 Inside information	• quotes from the director and the actors
7 Conclusion	• predictions about how popular it will be

This structure could help you to write an article to comment on a new film.

Comment: the designer of a film talking about the special effects

Paragraph and structure	Content
1 Introduction	• why the effects were needed • where they fitted in to the story
2, 3 Examples of special effects	• what they looked like • how they were achieved
4 A particularly complicated effect	• why it was difficult • how the problem was solved
5 Inside information	• quotes from the director and the actors
6 Conclusion	• the contribution that the special effects made to the success of the film

6 ▷ Looking back

- Remember the different approaches that you need to take when you are either **analysing**, **reviewing** or **commenting**.
- **Similes** and **metaphors** help to get ideas across in vivid and interesting ways.
- Different **genres** (of films or books) all have their own qualities which make them recognisable.

In the news

1 ▶ Purpose

In this unit you will:

- read pages from a news Web site
- study the three different kinds of articles: ones which analyse, review and comment
- create your own Web page and link articles

▶▶ **Subject links:** *history, art*

2 ▶ Writing to analyse, review and comment

Dunkirk remembered

June 2000 marked the sixtieth anniversary of a remarkable episode from the Second World War: the rescue of 338,000 British troops from the beaches of Dunkirk in northern France.

This news online Web site provided easy access to a wide range of articles about Dunkirk, all on pages easily visited from this Web page headed 'Dunkirk remembered'.

Here are three of the articles which could be accessed from this Dunkirk Web page. The first is an analysis, the second a review, the third a comment.

| Back | Forward | Home | Reload | Images | Print |

Location: http://onlinenews.co.uk

| What's New? | What's Cool? | Handbook | Net Search |

Front Page | **World** | **UK** | **UK Politics** | **Business** | **Talking Point** | **High Graphics** | **AudioVideo** | **Feedb**

UK Contents: **Northern Ireland** | **Scotland** | **Wales** |

ANALYSING DUNKIRK

Near the bottom of the 'Dunkirk remembered' Web page is a link to an article entitled 'The "miracle" of Dunkirk'. This turns out to be a helpful analysis of the historical facts.

Online News: UK

Tuesday, 30 May, 2000, 08:17 GMT 09:17 UK

The 'miracle' of Dunkirk

More than 300,000 troops were evacuated from Dunkirk and the surrounding beaches in May and June 1940. At the time the British Prime Minister Winston Churchill said it was 'a miracle of deliverance'. Dunkirk writer David J. Knowles explains what happened.

'A miracle' – is the best description of what happened at Dunkirk in May and June 1940.

Hundreds of thousands of troops were rescued from the jaws of the relentless German advance in the nick of time.

The troops were desperately needed back on the home shores to help defend against being invaded ourselves.

They were rescued from the harbour and beaches near to Dunkirk by a curious assembly of many different types of craft.

Many of the little ships, such as motor yachts, fishing boats and all manner of other such craft, were privately owned.

German forces underestimated

Although a large number of these ships were taken across the channel by navy personnel – many were also taken over by their owners and other civilians, all eager to help in what had become a catastrophe.

The British, French and Belgium governments had seriously underestimated the strength of the German forces in their equipment, transport and fire power – which was far superior to much of our outdated armoury.

Consequently the British Expeditionary Force, as well as the French and Belgian forces, found themselves defending positions against overwhelming odds.

Desperate retreat

Before long, with the Germans effectively cutting off nearly all of the escape routes to the channel, the BEF found itself desperately retreating to the harbour and beaches of Dunkirk.

Vice Admiral Ramsay – who was in charge of Operation Dynamo – had sent destroyers and transport ships to evacuate the troops, but they only expected to have time to lift off about 30,000 troops.

However, before long, the harbour became partially blocked by ships sunk in consistent attacks from enemy aircraft. It became necessary to take the troops off the nearby beaches as well – something that was thought to be an almost impossible task because of shallow water.

Seemed like a victory

This is when the little ships came to play their part. A variety of motor boats, fishing smacks, trawlers, lifeboats, paddle steamers and many other types of craft came over the Channel to assist in the escape.

They mainly ferried the troops from the beaches to the destroyers lying offshore – but thousands of troops came all the way back to England in some of these boats.

The escape captured the minds and hearts of the British people at a time when it looked probable that we too would soon be invaded.

It seemed like a victory in just getting the troops back – over a third of a million of them – to fight another day.

David J Knowles

- How many British troops were rescued from the beaches of Dunkirk? When did this happen?
- How did the Dunkirk harbour become blocked, making it difficult for large ships to get in?
- Why did the Dunkirk escape lift the sprits of the people back home?

> **REVIEWING WHAT PEOPLE SAY ABOUT DUNKIRK**
>
> *The feature entitled 'Lest we forget' consists mainly of a review of people's attitudes today to the Dunkirk story.*

| Back | Forward | Home | Reload | Images | Print | Find | Stop |

Location: http://onlinenews.co.uk

| What's New? | What's Cool? | Handbook | Net Search | Net Directory |

Front Page | World | UK | UK Politics | Business | Sci/Tech | Health | Education | Sport | Entertainment |
Talking Point | High Graphics | AudioVideo | Feedback | Help | Noticias | Newyddion |

UK Contents: Northern Ireland | Scotland | Wales |

Online News: UK

Monday, 15 May 2000, 17:48 GMT 18:48 UK

Dunkirk: Lest we forget

The veterans of Dunkirk may be ready to call time on their annual reunion, but the 60-year-old memories are still fresh for the soldiers plucked to safety in the daring rescue.

For young people in the UK today – many of whom have no firsthand experience of war – the evacuation is a ripping yarn at best, a complete mystery at worst.

Dunkirk spirit

The Dunkirk Veterans Association, set up after the war to care for the injured and to keep the Dunkirk spirit of endurance and co-operation alive, is soon to be disbanded as most of the surviving members are in their 80s.

On Monday, 55 veterans met for the final time at London's Imperial War Museum.

But while the men still clearly recall their ordeal, what do young people today think of this defining moment of British history? Clearly, keeping the memory of Dunkirk alive and relevant is proving to be an uphill challenge.

A survey by Online News found few young adults could pin down exactly what happened on 4 June 1940. But they did have strong views about whether the spirit of Dunkirk lived on.

'Everybody's self-centred these days. All they think about is themselves.' Michele Johnson, 15.

'I don't think that's right. People do still care about others.' Sam Bergfors, 17.

'Dunkirk? Is that in Scotland?' Mark, 14.

'I've never heard of him.' Jo, 16.

'That's when all those little boats went over and rescued the soldiers stuck in France.' Bill Mackintosh, 14.

'If they hadn't been saved, we'd have lost the war.' Dean, 16.

'One of our neighbours had been at Dunkirk and said how frightening it was – they were being attacked by planes all the time they were waiting to be picked up. They had nothing to eat either – he lived on maggots.' Jane Thompson, 16.

'My grandad was at Dunkirk. It's difficult to imagine what it was like – except what you see on the films.' Marianne Jones, 14.

'I was there. The main thing I remember is how everybody helped everyone else. And there was no panic either. We all waited and just took our turn when it came. It was the same when we got back, too. People kept giving us food and cups of tea.' Arthur Harrison, 82.

'Yes, I think people would do what we did if something like that happened again. The youngsters I know would, anyway.' George Jackson, 84.

- What is the name of the organisation originally set up to care for the injured of Dunkirk? How old were most of its members when they met up for the last time?

- What did the Online News survey reveal about young people's knowledge of Dunkirk?

- What were 82-year-old Arthur Harrison's main memories of Dunkirk and his return to England?

COMMENTING ON THE DUNKIRK SPIRIT

Another page has an article which asks the question: 'Dunkirk spirit: Do we still have it?' This comments on the British people and asks whether they still do possess the ability to keep fighting when things get tough.

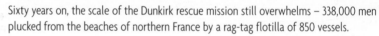

Back | Forward | Home | Reload | Images | Print | Find | Stop

Location: http://onlinenews.co.uk

What's New? | What's Cool? | Handbook | Net Search | Net Directory

Front Page | World | UK | UK Politics | Business | Sci/Tech | Health | Education | Sport | Entertainment |
Talking Point | High Graphics | AudioVideo | Feedback | Help | Noticias | Newyddion |

Special Report Contents: El Niño | Mars Surveyor probe | ISS | Unabomber | Mayor News | House of Lords |

Online News: In Depth: - e-cyclopedia

Thursday, 1 June 2000, 09:09 GMT 10:09 UK

Dunkirk spirit: Do we still have it?

Sixty years on, the scale of the Dunkirk rescue mission still overwhelms – 338,000 men plucked from the beaches of northern France by a rag-tag flotilla of 850 vessels.

A retreat it may have been, but the humiliation of defeat was more than tempered[1] by the triumph of what became known as 'Dunkirk spirit'.

But while Dunkirk remains a towering monument to British bravery, what of the spirit it spawned?

In short, does Dunkirk spirit still exist?

The spirit in question is the ability of British people to come together and rise above adversity.[2]

In his book, *50 Years On*, veteran labour politician Lord Hattersley notes how the immediate post-war years were characterised by a strong sense of 'all for one, one for all' community.

That fell to the mantra of individualism[3] championed by Margaret Thatcher, who famously commented 'there is no such thing as society'. Yet Lord Hattersley is certain Dunkirk spirit has survived into the 21st century.

'Of course it still exists. The British character is often at its best when its people are cornered and must fight their way out,' he says.

There has been little call for it in a wartime context. Since 1945, Britain has engaged in limited conflicts, often backed by the might of the Americans.

Inevitably, if Dunkirk spirit exists, it is in a tamer environment.

Sing your troubles away

The notoriously bad weather can bring out Britons' gritty determination. In 1996, Sir Cliff Richard stood up on centre court at Wimbledon during a downpour and convinced some 11,000 spectators to join him in an impromptu[4] sing-song.

Although they won't thank you for the comparison, Glastonbury festival-goers showed a similar defiance during the rain-lashed shows of 1997 and 1998.

Jacqui Gellman, of London's Regent's Park Open Air Theatre, says shows are frequently interrupted by showers, but audiences seldom complain.

'Sometimes when they are watching Shakespeare there are references to the weather and you get these great roars of laughter from the audience,' says Ms Gellman.

But Dunkirk spirit is not necessarily a laughing matter. Last year British consumers put on a show of solidarity by boycotting French produce after France refused to accept British beef imports.

The wave of public mourning for Diana, Princess of Wales, showed the British still have a capacity to come together in a time of crisis.

So 60 years on, there is plenty of evidence that Dunkirk spirit is still key to the British character.

Not everyone is happy though. Jasper Griegson, author of *The Complete Complainer*, says Dunkirk spirit is stopping us from getting what we really want.

'Faced with bad service, the British would rather button their lip and remain resolute than speak out,' says Mr Griegson. 'We should be very proud of what happened at Dunkirk but the problem is we are now too accustomed to losing.'

[1] more than tempered: *made less painful*
[2] adversity: *difficulties and misfortune*
[3] mantra of individualism: *repeated chant that people were individuals*
[4] impromptu: *unrehearsed and improvised*

---

3 **Key features**

News Web sites such as Online News contain a wide variety of reports and articles, including ones which analyse, review and comment on a particular news item.

- The analytical article explains the historical background and gives a summary of what happened at Dunkirk.
- The review article gives a sample of different people's views and responses.
- The third article is a collection of comments.

- How does this writer define 'the Dunkirk spirit' (in the fifth sentence)?
- According to Lord Hattersley, when is the British character 'often at its best'?
- Which three outdoor events are examples of the way in which British people refuse to be beaten by bad weather?

4 ⟩ Language skills

Word

An **adjective** is a word which helps to give more information about a noun or pronoun.

These Web pages contain a large number of adjectives which help the reader to understand the terrible situation that the British troops found themselves in and the heroism of the ordinary people who sailed across the Channel to help rescue them.

❶ Look back at the article entitled 'The "miracle" of Dunkirk'. Find the adjectives which describe the following nouns:

- the German *advance*
- the *assembly* of craft which had gathered to rescue the troops
- the *odds* against the British and allied forces
- the British *retreat*
- the *attacks* from enemy aircraft
- the *task* of rescuing the troops from the beaches.

Spelling

Computer technology has created a whole dictionary of new words. On Web sites like this one, words like *online*, *homepage* and *feedback* are all usually written without hyphens.

❶ Note the different endings in *audio* and *video*. Check their meanings.

❷ Note the newly invented word *e-cyclopedia*. How has it been formed?

❸ Which do you see most often in print these days: *e-mail*, *email* or *Email*?

Sentence

A **simple sentence** is one which contains only one clause.

The first article, 'The "miracle" of Dunkirk' contains a number of simple sentences. They are a good way to get the facts across directly and clearly.

❶ The first sentence (*More than...*) is a simple sentence. Write it down and underline the main verb.

❷ Do the same with the simple sentences beginning *Hundreds of thousands...* and *They were rescued...*

Text

The three articles on Dunkirk are examples of the three kinds of writing that you have studied in this book: writing to **analyse**, **review** and **comment**.

Writing to analyse uses facts and gives **explanations**. This kind of writing helps to answer questions such as: *Why are things as they are (or were)?*

1 Look back at the analyse article, 'The "miracle" of Dunkirk'. Write down three facts about:

- when the Dunkirk evacuation took place
- how many troops were involved
- the sort of privately owned ships that went to their aid

2 Write down the three explanations for:

- why the troops were in Dunkirk in the first place
- why they had to be taken off the beaches, rather than the harbour
- why Dunkirk came to seem like a victory

Writing to review uses people's **viewpoints**, attitudes and perspectives and offers **opinions**. It answers questions such as: *What is my (or her, his, their...) opinion of things?*

3 Write out in your own words the different feelings about Dunkirk that the following two groups might have:

- Dunkirk veterans
- young people in the UK today

Writing to **comment** uses **examples** in order to think through ideas and make **observations**. It answers questions such as: *What do I want to say about things?*

4 Look back at 'Dunkirk spirit: Do we still have it?' Note down the three examples of the 'Dunkirk spirit' that people saw in Wimbledon tennis, rock concerts and open-air theatre.

5 Complete the following three observations:

- *If the Dunkirk spirit still exists, it shows itself in...*
- *The recent example of the British coming together in time of crisis was...*
- *The Dunkirk spirit can be a problem because...*

5 ▷ Planning your own writing

Create a Web page for a subject in the news which interests you. Then create three link-pages: one which analyses the subject, one which reviews it and one which comments on it.

▶ STARTING POINT

- You will need to find a news item where there is plenty of background information; something to do with history or science will give you the kind of material you need.

- Use the three pages on Dunkirk as models.

- Visit a news Web site for ideas. You could try BBC News Online (*www.bbc.co.uk/news*) or Channel 4 news (*www.channel4news.co.uk*).

- The work will be easier and more interesting to do if you can use a word-processor.

▶ CLUES FOR SUCCESS

The main aims of this activity are:

- to help you learn how Web pages are organised

- to give you practice in the different types of writing – to analyse, review and comment

Therefore:

- don't spend too much time on the graphics (illustrations, artwork and lettering) – the written text is much more important

- keep the three link-pages fairly brief

▶ REDRAFTING AND IMPROVING

Look carefully at your Web page and link-pages. Check that:

- the Web page shows a wide range of news items and feature articles, including analysis, review and comment

- your link-pages are clear examples of the three different kinds of writing – to analyse, review and comment

6 ▷ Looking back

- **Adjectives** give information about nouns or pronouns.

- **Simple sentences** contain only one clause; they are useful in getting straightforward facts across clearly and directly.

- Each of the three different kinds of writing – to **analyse, review** and **comment** – has its own special qualities. Writing to analyse uses facts and gives explanations. Writing to review uses viewpoints and offers opinions. Writing to comment uses examples to make observations.

 **WRITING FRAME**

To start you off, here is a writing frame for a Web page on news to do with the fortieth anniversary of the first moon-landing (2009).

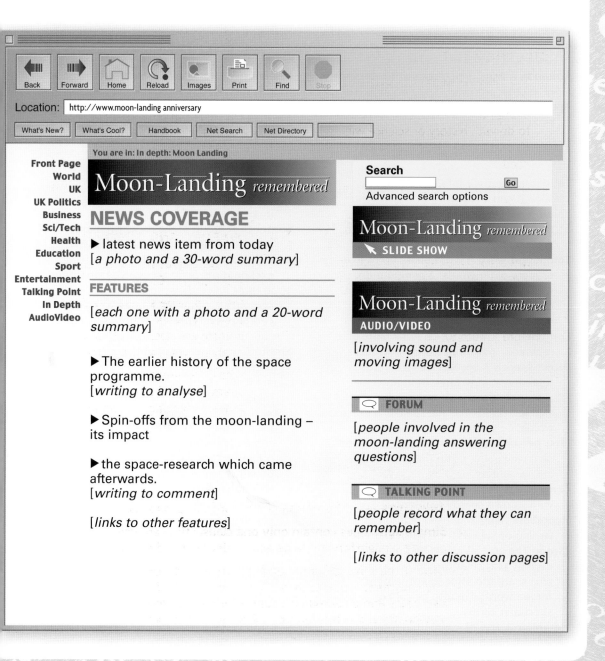

Glossary

Abstract noun The label we give to something we cannot touch, such as an emotion, feeling or idea.

Adjective A word which describes somebody or something. Adjectives help to give more information about a noun or pronoun.

Alliteration The repetition of consonant sounds to gain a particular effect.

Antonym A word which means the opposite of another word.

Apostrophe A punctuation mark (') with two different uses:
1 To show that a letter or group of letters has been missed out
2 To show possession (or ownership)

Colloquial English Informal, everyday speech and writing.

Colon A punctuation mark (:) which shows that there is something else to follow in the sentence, such as a list or an example.

Compound word A word made up of two or more other words. A compound word can be written down as one word, or with a hyphen if it looks confusing when written down.

Conjunction A word which joins parts of a sentence, individual words or phrases.

Direct speech A speaker's exact words reproduced in writing. In indirect (or reported) speech, we report what was said but do not use the speaker's exact words.

First person Writing something from your own viewpoint, using the pronouns *I*, *me*, *we* and *us*.

Genre A particular kind of writing or film with its own special features.

Hyperbole Deliberate exaggeration in writing or speech for a particular effect.

Jargon The special words and phrases used by particular groups of people who share the same job or interest. Jargon words can also be called **specialist terms**.

Metaphor A way of comparing things without using the words *like* or *as*, where the writer creates an image in the reader's mind and writes about something as if it really were something else.

Paragraph A block of sentences linked together by one main idea or subject.

Parenthesis A word or phrase inserted into a sentence to provide additional information, placed between commas, brackets or dashes.

Personification A special kind of metaphor in which things and ideas are spoken about as though they were people.

Prefix A group of letters added to the beginning of a word to change its meaning.

Semicolon A punctuation mark (;) which provides a stronger break than a comma. It can be used to join two main clauses in a sentence.

Sentence A group of words which makes sense. A sentence can be a **statement**, a **question**, a **command** or an **exclamation**. Sentences can be structured in three ways: they can be **simple sentences**, **compound sentences** and **complex sentences**. A **simple sentence** contains only one clause.

Simile A way of comparing things in an unusual or unexpected way, in which the writer creates an image in the reader's mind. A simile uses the words *like* or *as*.

Speech marks (or **inverted commas**) are used to mark the beginning and end of someone's actual words when they are quoted in a piece of writing. They can be either single (' ') or double (" "). When they are used to show that a word or phrase is being quoted from somewhere else, they are known as **quotation marks**.

Synonym A word which means the same, or almost the same, as another word.

Tense The form of the verb which shows when something happens – either the past or the present or the future.

Wordplay The games that people play with words in order to achieve a special effect.